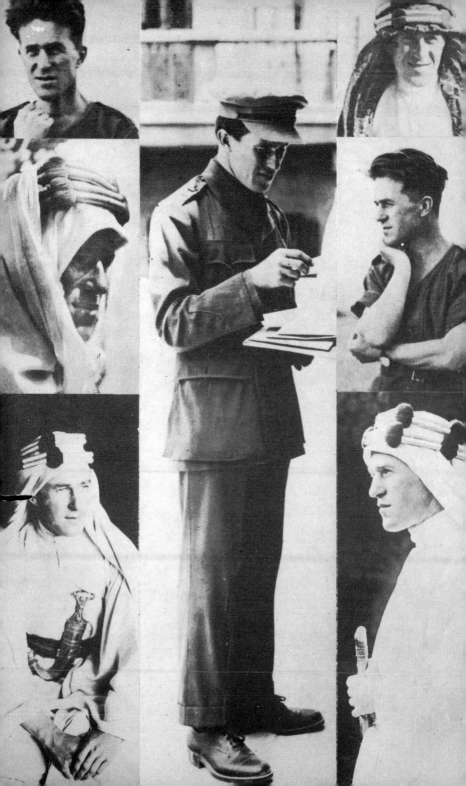

# Lawrence

**Douglas Orgill**

BB

Editor-in-Chief: Barrie Pitt
Editor: David Mason
Art Director: Sarah Kingham
Picture Editor: Robert Hunt
Consultant Art Editor: Dennis Piper
Designer: Sarah Kingham
Illustration: Owen Wood
Photographic Research: Carina Dvorak
Cartographer: Richard Natkiel

First Printing:   May   1973
Printed in United States of America

Ballantine Books Inc.
101 Fifth Avenue New York NY 10003

# Contents

# Charisma...
## Introduction by Barrie Pitt

The word might have been invented to fit T. E. Lawrence. Few other men in out time have possessed the ability to cast such a spell upon those they wished to influence; few have at the same time been held in such wide, popular esteem in many countries. There was a surprisingly large number of people in both Europe and America who refused to believe, for many months, that Lawrence had in fact died as a result of the accident on 13th May 1935.

What qualities went into the making of such a legend?

Firstly, there was undoubtedly tremendous force of will, driving its owner to feats of physical endurance which appal the imagination, and other men to success in tasks for which they seemed to have little taste or even aptitude. Secondly, there was great intellectual force. His writings, from the translation of Homer to *The Mint*, including even *Seven Pillars of Wisdom* and especially his letters, reveal a power of concentration and a depth of perception which is impressive at all times and, at its best, far beyond the reach of most of us. His analysis of the strengths and weaknesses of the Arab Revolt and the resulting conclusions as to the most effective way to use it, was a remarkable feat for any soldier while actually engaged upon operations – let alone while in the grip of fever and suffering extreme discomfort from boils; most people like Job, would have spent the time bemoaning their fate. His conduct of the Battle of Tafila too, was far more an intellectual exercise on his part than an affair of gallantry. Thirdly, there was the force of personality which deeply impressed such men as Feisal, Winston Churchill, Bernard Shaw, Sir Basil Liddell Hart, Robert Graves and hundreds of private soldiers of diverse races and services — and indeed, was sufficient to persuade even General Sir Edward Allenby that the unsoldierly and unorthodox rabble on his right flank could materially aid his advance to Damascus.

So much for the qualities which raised Lawrence to eminence; other men have possessed such qualities and performed comparable deeds but remained only briefly in the public eye. How and why did Lawrence remain for so long and object of public regard and curiosity?

He had an amazing capacity for 'backing into the limelight'. Presumably he had no direct responsibility for that series of lectures on 'Lawrence of Arabia' given by the American journalist Lowell Thomas which first catapulted him into public renown – but he certainly appears to have made

6

capital from them. On one occasion, having sat inconspicuously among the audience for most of the lecture, he rose to his feet and stalked the length of the hall, shortly after a whole series of slides shown on the screen had made it virtually impossible for anyone in the audience not to recognise him.

His insistence on serving in the ranks of both the Royal Air Force and the Tank Corps was a continual topic of speculation in the Press, and his behaviour in the ranks a source of irritation and embarrassment to his superiors. Even towards the end of his service with the RAF, when both parties were to a great extent reconciled to each other, he caused embarrassment and annoyance. During the Schneider Trophy races off Calshot he spent time when he should have been on duty talking to such notables as Winston Churchill and Basil Liddell Hart. The fact that he was wearing the uniform of an air-craftsman amid such company, while officers laboured at their tasks, could hardly avoid comment. One cannot help thinking that, he had really desired the anonymity he professed, he would have done better to become a subaltern or a junior administrative officer in the RAF. God knows, there are few forms of life better calculated to fulfil his expressed wish to escape all recognition or responsibility.

Attempts to explain the enigma have been legion, but perhaps that put forward by Sir John Bagot Glubb – which has at least the advanatge that its author has vast experience of the physical and moral obstacles which Lawrence overcame in the days of his greatest achievements – comes nearest. 'Any analysis of Lawrence's psychology' he writes, 'must recognise first of all that he was the possessor of an extraordinary clear, versatile and penetrating intellect. This intellectual genius enabled him to see more clearly than most men; it also inspired him with an intellectual pride and a contempt for those less gifted, which often took the form of rudeness and arrogance which is difficult to excuse. The same penetrating intellect, however, enabled him also to appreciate the baseness and stupidity of most men, the vulgarity of the ambitious careerist and the futility of worldly titles and honours. Thus he renounced them because his mind was clear enough to see their vanity.'

If Sir John is right, it is fortunate for most of us that we do not possess Lawrence's gifts.

# The man

George Bernard Shaw, writing in the 1930s, remarked that British people in general knew only one tenth as much about their Prime Ministers as they did about T E Lawrence. Scholar, soldier, poet, author, guerilla leader, even technician, Lawrence sometimes appeared in the years after the First World War to be all things to all men. Winston Churchill called him 'one of the greatest beings of our time'; Basil Liddell Hart compared him with Marlborough, and was willing to place him among the Great Captains of history. In later years, there have been harsher judgments. The Arab historian, Suleiman Mousa, summed up his study of Lawrence by saying that 'deep within himself, Lawrence knew that the greater part of his fame was based on fraud'; the British biographer, Richard Aldington, decided that 'an immense legend was fabricated, largely by himself, from materials of uncertain substance . . .' All these verdicts are extreme, and all are clouded by differing reactions to Lawrence's powerful and complex personality. Legends should always be investigated, but their origins – and this applies especially to military legends – are rarely founded completely upon deceit.

Thomas Edward Lawrence was born on 16th August 1888 at Tremadoc in Wales. He was illegitimate – the second of five sons of Sir Thomas Chapman, a baronet, of West Meath in Ireland. His mother was Sarah Maden, a governess to the four daughters born to Sir Thomas by his wife Edith. Chapman's association with Sarah Maden led him in 1884 to leave his wife. He changed his name to Lawrence, set up house with Sarah Maden, and the couple settled finally, after some vicissitudes, in Oxford. They lived together until his death in 1919, married in all but name.

'Ned', as T E Lawrence was called by the rest of the family, went with his brothers to Oxford High School. Contemporaries remembered him later as a quiet boy, uninterested in school games, determined to be different, and with a liking for creating an unconventional reputation. He was small in stature, a little under five feet six inches when full-grown, and with a head that seemed rather big for his body. He was not by instinct a family boy. When he was seventeen, he ran away to join the Royal Artillery as a gunner, only to be promptly bought out by his father, who planned that he should go to Oxford University. He tried for an Oxford scholarship in 1906, and was turned down by St John's College, but won a history exhibition at Jesus College the following year.

Oxford has always been a breeding ground for amiable eccentricity, and it duly provided the right conditions for Lawrence to cultivate his reputation as an 'Original', though one of a

**Lawrence with Leonard Woolley on an archaeological dig in Syria, in 1910**

studiedly unflamboyant kind. Looking over Lawrence's time at the University, one can see many of the characteristics which were to develop to full fruition during the Arab Revolt and in the years after the war – the liking for unconventional adventure, as when he navigated the city's underground sewers in a canoe; the mortification of the body, exemplified by solemnly sitting in college hall one evening a week and eating nothing, and by his habit of riding his bicycle uphill and pushing it down; the scholarly interest in war, which drew him to his thesis on the military architecture of the Crusades, sent him to travel in Arabia, and thus eventually contributed to changing the history of the world. In all these activities, the observer can discern one particular feature: Lawrence cared little for the plaudits of the mob, but greatly for the esteem and admiration of a carefully-chosen circle. Over these he seemed sometimes to be able to exercise an almost hypnotic compulsion to believe what was said about him, even when rational reflection or cool analysis of time and place would clearly have made some of the stories impossible. He was certainly an omnivorous reader, but it has been pointed out that the claim that he had read 'the best part' of the 50,000 books in the Oxford Union Library meant that he would have read twenty-five a day for 2,000 days. Again, he was an adventurous and perceptive traveller in the Arab lands, but he did not go farther afield. Yet we find Lowell Thomas, the American writer who met Lawrence during the war, saying that 'at one time the British Museum sent him (Lawrence) on a short expedition to Sumatra, where he had escapes from headhunters almost as thrilling as his adventures in Arabia. But of these we could never persuade him to speak. Some day, perhaps, he may tell us of them in his memoirs . . .' The implication is clear that Lawrence had at least hinted strongly at these 'adventures', though they were purely imaginary. Lawrence never visited Sumatra in his life.

Paradoxically enough, however, this purposeful manipulation of the facts, varying from stretching the truth to complete fabrication of incidents,

The orientalists Lawrence met at the Ashmolean Museum: *Left:* D G Hogarth, the Museum Keeper; *Centre:* Leonard Woolley, the archaeologist; *Right:* C M Doughty well known for his Arabian travels

The Ashmolean Museum in Oxford, where Lawrence spent a great deal of his time and made the contacts which crystalised his interest in the East

was a quality which served him well in dealing with Arabs. Legend is highly important to a guerilla leader, and the ability to construct legend would one day help to make Lawrence a guerilla leader of genius — perhaps the greatest in British history.

Lawrence decided to offer a thesis for his Bachelor of Arts degree. He chose as his subject the influence of the Crusades on mediaeval military architecture. His interest in mediaeval warfare had already led him, according to his own later account, to visit 'every twelfth century castle in France, England and Wales', but his new thesis was now to take him to the Middle East. At Oxford, much of Lawrence's time was spent at the Ashmolean Museum, and his activities and research had brought him to the attention of three of the most celebrated orientalists of their day. They were the Keeper of the Museum himself, D G Hogarth, the archaeologist, Leonard Woolley, and C M Doughty, possibly the most famous and perceptive of British travellers in Arabia. The influence of these men in shaping Lawrence's future cannot be over-estimated. In the case of Hogarth, it was a deliberate, conscious influence, as we shall see – though Hogarth himself can hardly have foreseen, in the summer of 1909, the destiny to which his young *protégé* would be drawn within a decade.

In 1909, Hogarth was forty-seven. An archaeologist of great distinction, a correspondent for *The Times*, a Fellow of Magdalen College, he seems to modern eyes to have something of the *charisma* of a character in a John Buchan novel, and his activities sometimes had a John Buchan-ish flavour. He was, in fact, part of the strange half-intellectual, half-adventurous establishment, firmly based in the upper middle class, which lay behind the concept of continuing Empire. In the first decade of the 20th Century, this was still the greatest driving force in British minds. Thus Hogarth was not formally a member of British Intelligence, but intelligence experts listened to his opinions with respect. They read his papers and, on occasion, used him to recruit help abroad, or even to keep an eye on subjects of interest within his field of specialised knowledge. That field of knowledge embraced the Ottoman Empire and the Arab lands. It was into the general area of these somewhat amorphous activities that Hogarth gradually introduced Lawrence in the coming years.

Doughty was a figure of an altogether different kind. He was a celebrated traveller, and an epic poet, but his most famous work was his *Travels in Arabia Deserta*, a record – set down in a monumental, quasi-Elizabethan English – of a journey undertaken in 1876 through unknown parts of Arabia. Doughty's influence on Lawrence was not of a personal nature, like Hogarth's, although he both met and corresponded with Lawrence. It was Doughty's book which fired Lawrence's imagination, and it was the intention to produce a book of his own which drove Lawrence forward in later years. Doughty's own description of his book was that it 'is not milk for babes: it might be likened to a mirror, wherein is set forth faithfully some parcel of the soil of Arabia . . .' Lawrence himself said of it that 'it is not comfortable to have to write about *Arabia Deserta*. I have studied it for ten years, and have grown to consider it a book not like other books, but something particular, a bible of its kind . . .' Thus even before the war began in 1914, both Hogarth and Doughty, in very different ways, had begun to guide this unusual young man to his strange future.

In pursuit of material for his thesis, Lawrence set out on a journey through Syria and Palestine in the summer of 1909. He had learned some Arabic in lessons from an Oxford clergyman, and he travelled on foot, beginning the considerable feats of physical endurance which were to become characteristic of his Arabian existence. He visited thirty-six castles, sketching, photographing, and measuring, walking through the ancient Syrian places of Baalbek and down the Jordan valley to Nazareth and Haifa. He had several attacks of malaria – possibly a recurrence of the form of the disease which he had picked up a year or two earlier while on a similar expedition through the Camargue marshes of Provence. But the result was a thesis (later published as *Crusader Castles*) which gained him a first-class honours degree, and hardened Hogarth's interest in him. It was, indeed, Hogarth's recommendation which secured him a research scholarship at Magdalen College, so that he could afford to join, unpaid, the British Museum archaeological dig on the Hittite site at Carchemish, on the River Euphrates.

Lawrence was not more than an ordinarily useful archaeologist. His dislike for routine work was a disadvantage in following an activity which was rapidly becoming more and more scientific, and yet it has been said, probably with truth, that the next two years were the happiest of his life. He learned a lot about how Arabs thought and acted, and also something about how his own body responded to desert conditions. The work at Carchemish was later directed by Leonard Woolley, and Lawrence was in charge of the pottery section of the dig, as well as of the photography.

From the outset, he was extraordinarily successful at handling the 200 Arab and Kurdish workers employed at the dig. He had learned the first lesson of leadership – that the leader must be of his men, yet apart from them, must be instantly recognisable to them in his way of life, yet able to withdraw into areas of decision where they could not follow him. He brought to the direction of these archaeological diggers a considerable psychological insight – one which he seems to have possessed especially in relation to Arabs. While he settled their disputes, joined in their jokes, listened to their talk, he arrived at a clear assessment of the nature of the people he was dealing with.

'Their thoughts live easiest among extremes', he wrote later. 'They inhabit superlatives by choice ... They exclude compromise, and pursue the logic of their ideas to its absurd ends, without seeing incongruity in their opposed conclusions. They are a people of spasms, of upheavals, of ideas, the race of the individual genius ... Their convictions are by instinct, their activities intuitional ...'

It was at Carchemish that Lawrence also began his friendship with an Arab water-boy, a handsome fair lad whose name was Sheik Ahmed, though he was nicknamed Dahoum. This association does not appear to have been homosexual in the commonly accepted sense of the word. An English friend of this period described Lawrence perceptively as 'sexless ... at least, he was unaware of sex ...' The friendship with Dahoum, who was to die of typhoid within a few years, was probably the most serious and intense relationship Lawrence ever had with another human being, and there is good ground for believing that Dahoum, or Sheik Ahmed, was the mysterious 'S A' to whom Lawrence dedicated the despairing little poem at the beginning of his book *Seven Pillars of Wisdom*.

As the first decade of the 20th Century ended, then, we find this odd, clever, self-absorbed and somewhat emotionally immature young man facing a future which must have seemed to him to be vague and hard to plan. Like many young men, he had stirrings that some sort of destiny beckoned, though what it could be was impossible to discern. He had done something to prepare his body, and much to prepare his mind. He disliked the hard slog of routine: in that respect he was rather like an Arab. He had the ability and imagination to play a part in affairs: he had, in Hogarth, an important patron. What he needed now was a stage.

# The stage

The Turks, in the shape of the Ottoman Empire, had ruled the Middle East for four centuries. The Empire was a creaking, ramshackle structure, loosely linked by the broad common faith of Islam, but condemned sixty years before by a Russian Czar as 'the sick man of Europe'. Even before 1914, the Middle East was becoming a cockpit for the four great powers, Britain, France, Russia and Germany. Yet there were stirrings deeper still than these alien interests. The Arab peoples of the lands which now comprise Syria, Lebanon, Jordan, Israel and Saudi Arabia, the whole of the Arabian peninsula, were restive. Beneath the veneer of religious unity, revolt was simmering against the Turks. Turkish control of this great area was often no more than nominal; only in the great towns such as Baghdad or Damascus did Turkish garrisons adequately buttress Turkish political power.

This was especially true of the great land mass of Arabia, flanked on three sides by the Persian Gulf, the Red Sea and the Indian Ocean, and in the north by the deserts of Jordan. It is the largest land peninsula in the world and about half of it is desert. Over most of Arabia, the mean annual rainfall does not reach more than an inch —compared with the forty-odd inches of temperate Europe. The population of Arabia – an area of 1,200,000 square miles – was in 1914 less than 7,000,000. In general, the land was stern, harsh and demanding – a land where whether in the coastal plain of the Hejaz along the line of the Red Sea, or the northern upland desert of Nejd, or the great furnace-beaten stretch of the central Rub-al-Khali, the Empty Quarter, only the greatest endurance and ability to adapt to fierce physical conditions enabled human life to prosper.

If the main *dramatis personae* of

Turks in Damascus; the Ottoman
Empire was now being threatened by
internal rebellion

British interest in the Middle East
extends to reorganising the Egyptian
army

Protection of her Middle Eastern oil
supplies was one of a number of motives
behind Britain's manoeuvrings in the
area

the desert were the sun, the camel and
the date-palm, undoubtedly the classic hero of this stage was the Bedouin.
It was he who represented a successful
human adaptation of means to ends in
this cruel world. The Bedouin had to
fight against his environment from
the day he was born: thus he has become, above all, an individualist,
never able to submit himself to the
comfort and the demands of a large
social or national organisation. The
family and the tribe were the only
social units to which he paid respect
and allegiance: the camel was his
wealth. He wore its skin, drank its
milk, ate its flesh, built his tents
from its hair. Above all, he bred it
for speed and endurance – and it was
his vehicle for war. Tribal warfare,
for these small, fragmented desert
units – often only loosely united
under some more general tribal name
– was an essential part of the annual
economy. It was not war which
was costly in human lives – a handful
of Bedouin killed in such an affray
would provide endless material for
a Bedouin poet to sing around a
campfire for generations. It was war
conducted for water and for grazing –
and as a means of educating Bedouin
youth to its responsibilities in the
forbidding world which stretched
around it. Especially, it was mobile
war – conducted swiftly, stealthily,
striking through a desert dawn, a
flurry of shots or stabbing lances, a
shout, a scream, and then a with-
drawal back into the empty desert.
Mobility was all. The Bedouin was a
tough, formidable fighting man, but
his very virtues in this respect would
make it difficult for him to think in a
modern military regimental way.
And, obviously, this was not a society
over which a few Turkish garrisons
could exercise any very effective
control.

German aid in bringing the Turkish army up to date is extended, in 1913, by the appointment of General Liman von Sanders as head of a new military mission to Constantinople

An encampment on the Suez Canal in 1915. In January of this year the Turks attacked from the east and reached the Canal before being forced to retreat by the British garrison

In human terms, the Bedouin gloried in his poverty and austerity, and thought himself, with his carefully nurtured family pedigree, to be the aristocrat of the earth. He had come to terms with the desert. Lawrence himself tells a story of how, in Syria before the war, he had ridden with his friend Dahoum to a Roman ruin which was said to have had various perfumes absorbed into its building clay. The two had wandered from room to ruined room, fancying that they could smell rose, violet, jasmine, until Dahoun drew him to the window and asked him to smell 'the sweetest smell of all'. It was the desert wind, eddying all the way from the distant Euphrates. 'This', Lawrence was told, 'is best. It has no taste'. These were the men and this was the land which was now to be caught up in the great explosion of the First World War.

British interest in the Middle East was complex and considerable. Further east lay the great empire of India, incomparably the most important British imperial possession. The short route to India was the Suez Canal, and Egypt, though still in name a Turkish province, was in effect a British protectorate, effec-tively ruled by a British consul general. Britain could not afford to allow any other European power to attain to dominance in the Middle East, for the areas of Syria, Palestine and Arabia were vital manoeuvring grounds for the defence of India. There was also – less vital than today, but growing in importance – the question of oil. The Anglo-Persian Oil Company, whose oilfields were the only important ones in the Middle East, could be barred from using its tankers if the Turks closed the straits of the Shatt al-Arab on the Persian Gulf.

In the first decade of the 20th century, Kaiser Wilhelm's Germany was also looking east. Germany had both political and economic designs on Mesopotamia, which the Kaiser vaguely dreamed of turning into an exclusive sphere of interest, culmi-

Part of the Canal's defence rests on trench systems

Lawrence (with Commander Hogarth) in Cairo. He and Woolley there set up an intelligence office in December 1914

nating in a protectorate. Britain's new *entente* with Russia gave the Germans a chance. It had struck a heavy blow at Turkish friendship with Britain, for Russia was the traditional bogeyman for the Turks. The Germans had for some years been helping to modernise the Turkish army – a process which was quickened by the nationalist Young Turk revolution in 1908. Five years later, in 1913, General Liman von Sanders arrived in Constantinople at the head of a new German military mission. It was hardly surprising that at this point the eyes of British military intelligence were fixed on the Sinai, the stretch of desert peninsula under Turkish control, which lay east of the Suez Canal and provided an approach to it from Palestine.

The Sinai was virtually unmapped. Lawrence was now drawn into much more precise intelligence activities, for he was one of a party sent to this overtly Turkish area in order to prepare military maps. The job appears

to have been found for him by the enigmatic Hogarth: he was accompanied by his friend, Dahoum, and his chief, Woolley. The whole operation was under the command of Captain S F Newcombe, of the Royal Engineers, and it was nominally carried out under the auspices of the respectable Palestine Exploration Fund, which was said to be seeking information about Israelite journeys during the forty years spent in the desert. The report on this reconnaissance by Lawrence's party was later published as the *Wilderness of Zin*.

Europe went to war in August 1914. At the end of October, Turkey declared war on Russia. Lawrence was twenty-six years old: with his experience in the Arab lands, it was natural that he was now employed, commissioned as a second lieutenant, in general intelligence work in Egypt. Thus he fortunately avoided the man-consuming Western Front, where two of his brothers were soon to be killed.

General Townsend, who surrendered with his army at Kut-el-Amara when Lawrence's attempt to buy their freedom had failed

He completed his work on the Sinai maps. This was of considerable importance, incidentally, since the Turks attacked across the desert during the winter of 1914, reaching the Canal with 20,000 men by January 1915. They were rebuffed by a strong British garrison, and eventually retired into Palestine with a loss of about a tenth of their force.

In December 1914, Lawrence, Newcombe and Woolley were given the task of setting up in an intelligence department in Cairo. Lawrence's job was a curious one. In effect, he was a liaison officer providing a link between military intelligence authorities – some of which were later constituted into the Arab Bureau – and the Survey of Egypt, a civil department of the Egyptian administration, which was primarily concerned with map-making and topographical information. It was work of which he had good knowledge, but it could hardly be called the sort of destiny of which a man might dream. Lawrence was fascinated by war, but he was not in any sense a regimental officer, and he possessed neither the good points nor the bad points of a regimental mind. He was not popular with regular soldiers in Cairo – behaving in a way which his friends called impish and his enemies called spoilt. Ernest Dowson, who headed the Survey of of Egypt at this time, remembered Lawrence later as an 'extremely youthful and, to our unseeing eyes, insignificant figure with well-ruffled light hair, solitary pip on sleeve, minus belt and with peaked cap askew, riding out on his motorcycle Boanerges . . .' But within a few months, although many disliked him, he had won a wary admiration from those who worked with him closely. Dowson, again, said of him that 'he rapidly earned the respect of a very varied and specialist staff, because of his quickness in understanding technical details, and his appreciation of the

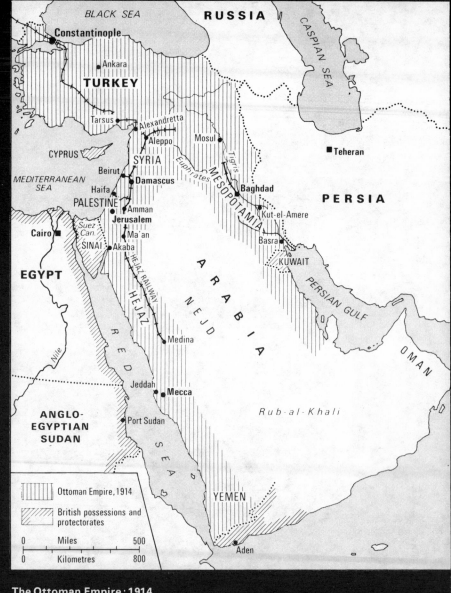

**The Ottoman Empire: 1914**

difficulties and limitations of the different processes of map and book production. Those who dealt with him continuously are agreed that it stands out prominently in their memories that they were always encountering some new side to his knowledge and capacity . . .' Lawrence, in fact, was far from being simply the spoiled, mocking undergraduate-officer that many of the regular officers at Cairo headquarters believed him to be. A Syrian official who was interviewed by Lawrence at this time also recalled later the impression of competence which he projected: 'We were received by an officer, who was short, fair-haired, with a large head and a small body, a rectangular face, and blue fiery eyes in constant motion. . . . As he talked to us we noticed that he looked at our faces only furtively, and that he spoke in near-whispers, with a reticence that aroused our caution; but his conversation was precise, profound and searching, which indicated a subtle mind and a thorough grasp of the subject . . .'

Even allowing, however, for the undoubted abilities which intelligent observers were able to distinguish behind Lawrence's nervous giggle and annoyingly mocking facade, the next step in his career is surprising. He was suddenly entrusted with a mission of great importance and delicacy – nothing less than an attempt to buy the freedom of General Townsend's surrounded British army which was beseiged in Kut-el-Amara, on the road to Baghdad. Lawrence was now a captain, but such a junior officer was a most unexpected choice for such an important operation. The order came direct from the War Office in London, and it is impossible not to see in it the hand of Hogarth, who was soon to exercise even more direct influence as director of the Arab Bureau. Accompanied by a British MP, Aubrey Herbert, who was also a captain in intelligence, Lawrence set off with 1,000,000 at his disposal in an attempt, to quote his orders, 'if possible to purchase one of the leaders of the Mesopotamian Army such as Khalil or Negib so as to facilitate the relief of Townsend . . .' The mission was unsuccessful. Khalil Pasha, the Turkish commander, spurned the British offer, and Townsend, starved of supplies, surrendered. Lawrence's sharply critical report did little to endear him to the high command in Cairo. Nevertheless, his sudden transition to these high affairs of state must have convinced many that he had important friends, and was a man of greater weight than had hitherto been supposed.

Lawrence's questing intelligence – undoubtedly his most outstanding characteristic to those who came to know him well – was already driving him to seek employment far removed from the comparatively trivial duties of a staff captain in Cairo. He was now talking regularly to Turkish prisoners and to travellers from Palestine and Mesopotamia. He had no experience, training or aptitude for commanding a platoon or a company in battle. But he had the ability to recognise sooner than most that something important was stirring among the Arab peoples, something which could be turned to account for Britain in this long and bitter war. It was politics rather than battle which now occupied the attention of this singular junior officer at his desk in Cairo.

Any revolt in Arabia against Turkish rule must have the religious backing of the legitimate forces of Islam. To do this, the Sultan of Turkey must be deprived of his spiritual leadership, and replaced as Caliph by someone willing to lead the revolt. Lawrence had already, in his own mind, selected the candidate for this crucial position. During 1916, he had been working on a memorandum called *The Conquest of Syria*, and his choice had fallen on the Sherif of Mecca, Husein, a descendant of the Prophet Mohammed. Husein was an imperious and self-seeking old man with no love for the Turks. Lawrence

Husein, Sherif of Mecca, rides with his entourage. He was Lawrence's choice of leader for an Arab revolt against the Turks

wrote of him in his memorandum: 'This war should, if it resulted in anything at all, take away finally and definitely the religious supremacy of the Sultan . . . The most probable claiment . . . would be the Sherif of Mecca . . . He is held down by Turkish money – which we, via Egypt or India could replace with interest – and by a Turkish Army Corps. The only way to rid ourselves of this (hostilities in the Yemen being impossible) is by cutting the Hedjaz (railway) line. The soldiers are paid and supplied with arms, etc., along this line, and its existence is always a present threat of reinforcements. By cutting it, we destroy the Hedjaz civil government . . . and we resolve the Hedjaz (Turkish) army into its elements – an assembly of peaceful Syrian peasants and incompetent alien officers. The Arab chiefs in the Hedjaz would then make their own play . . . The Bedouin tribes hate the railway which has reduced their annual tolls and way-leaves; and would help us cut it. The cutting could be done by occupying Deraa if Damascus is neutralised: at Amman, if Jerusalem can be passed, by blowing up a viaduct: and at Maan by an occupation . . .'

This remarkable document, drawn up largely when Lawrence was still a lieutenant, helps to establish him as a classic guerilla leader. It contains all the vital ingredients for the role: an acute assessment of the basic – in this case, religious – situation; a keen eye for the map and the topographical possibilities; and, above all, a clear appreciation of the motives that would actuate the Bedouin, who must form the actual instrument with which Lawrence's aims could be achieved, Even while Lawrence still sat in Cairo, the rough masterplan for a British-influenced Arab revolt was developing in his mind.

# The mission

In October 1916, Lawrence – probably because of his clear-sighted memorandum, and possibly also because he was unpopular at headquarters – succeeded in getting himself sent to accompany Ronald Storrs, Oriental Secretary to the British Agency in Egypt, on a mission to Jedda, the port of Mecca. The Arabs in the Hedjaz had already risen against the scanty Turkish forces in the area. As Lawrence had predicted, they were led by Husein. He had a force of around 50,000 Arabs, mainly Bedouin tribesmen, but it was an army in little more than name. 'Practically a rabble, and run on Dervish lines', was the judgment of one British military observer who examined the forces of the Sherif. There were fewer than 10,000 rifles for this host, and the Arabs had neither artillery nor machine guns. Against these, though in scattered outposts, the Turks could range 15,000 men in good defensive positions, reasonably well equipped to fight contemporar[y] war.

Yet the revolt had begun in a glow [of] success. Mecca fell after the Ara[b] forces succeeded in cutting off i[ts] water supply, and the Turks los[t] much of the southern area of th[e] Hedjaz, together with some of th[e] coastal towns. However, the Turk[s] retreated into the city of Medin[a] where, well-supplied with ammun[i-] tion, food and water, they held o[n]. They were sustained by the long lin[e] of the Hedjaz railway, since the Arab[s] simply did not have the technic[al] know how to blow the line and wrec[k] the trains. From Medina, the Turkis[h] force, commanded by Fakhri Pash[a,] mounted a perpetual threat to th[e] Arab-occupied city of Mecca. Arab[s] are not patient siege troops, and the[ir] fissiparous, tribal tendencies wer[e] already leading men to slip away fro[m] Husein's dwindling force. It was und[er] these circumstances that Storrs saile[d]

Though heavily outnumbered, the Turkish forces are very much better equipped than the Arab fighters

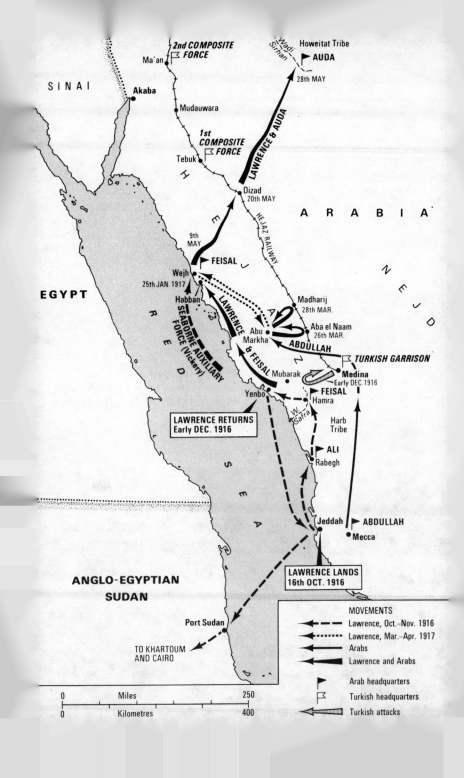

**2nd COMPOSITE FORCE**

Ma'an

**SINAI**

**Akaba**

Mudauwara

**1st COMPOSITE FORCE**

Tebuk

Dizad
20th MAY

9th MAY

**FEISAL**

Wejh
25th JAN. 1917

Habban

**SEABORNE AUXILIARY FORCE (Vickery)**

**EGYPT**

Wadi Sirhan

Howeitat Tribe
**AUDA**
28th MAY

**LAWRENCE & AUDA**

**ARABIA**

HEJAZ RAILWAY

**NEJD**

Madharij
28th MAR.

Aba el Naam
26th MAR.

Abu Markha

**ABDULLAH**

**LAWRENCE & FEISAL**

Mubarak

**TURKISH GARRISON**

Medina
Early DEC. 1916

**FEISAL**

Yenbo

Hamra

W. Safra

**LAWRENCE RETURNS**
Early DEC. 1916

Harb Tribe

**ALI**
Rabegh

**RED SEA**

**ANGLO-EGYPTIAN SUDAN**

Jeddah ▶ **ABDULLAH**
Mecca

**LAWRENCE LANDS**
16th OCT. 1916

Port Sudan

TO KHARTOUM AND CAIRO

**MOVEMENTS**
◄── ─ ─ Lawrence, Oct.–Nov. 1916
◄······ Lawrence, Mar.–Apr. 1917
◄─── Arabs
◄━━━ Lawrence and Arabs

▶ Arab headquarters
Ƀ Turkish headquarters
⟩━━━ Turkish attacks

| 0 | Miles | 250 |
| 0 | Kilometres | 400 |

n the 2,000-ton converted merchant-man *Lama* for the Arab-controlled port of Jedda, accompanied, as he noted in his diary, by 'little Lawrence, my super-cerebral companion'. His mission was to see what could be done to prop up and encourage the enterprise which Husein had begun.

Storrs and Lawrence landed at Jeddah on the 16th, and were met by the second of Husein's four sons, Abdulla (who was much later to become Emir and then King Abdullah of Jordan). Although Lawrence was officially little more than a super-numary in Storrs' party – he was, in fact, actually spending a leave on the trip – it was thenceforward that his part in the Arab Revolt began. Storrs, of course, was at that moment in time infinitely the more important of the two: it is notable that his contemporary diary has little to say of Lawrence other than as an interesting companion. On Lawrence's own estimate, Storrs was 'the most brilliant Englishman in the Near East', and yet it was not long before Lawrence's driving intelligence and impressive memory began to make their impact. Much later, Storrs wrote of the meeting with Abdullah: 'How instinctively he (Lawrence) played his cards when first presented to the Sherif Abdullah at Jeddah. We sat in a circle and the conversation was led up to the whereabouts of the various Turkish regiments – which was, of course, pooled and common knowledge of Lawrence's department, and for which King Husein had his own contacts of accurate information. As Syrian, Circassian, Anatolian, Mesopotamian names came up, Lawrence at once stated exactly which unit was in which position, until Abdullah turned to me in amazement: 'Is this man God, to know everything . . .?'

Lawrence, indeed, was now beginning to show his hand, and a very ambitious hand it was for such a junior officer. 'I went down to Arabia,' he wrote later, 'to see and consider its great men'. He was looking for an effective leader for the Arab Revolt – a name which he could later put forward in Cairo.

Husein and his four sons were the only practicable group from whom such a leader could be found, and Lawrence turned them over one by one in his mind. Husein, he knew already, was too old and too mulish. He was not happy about Ali's health or Zeid's staying power. He did not like Abdullah, and for that matter, Abdullah did not like him. With his strangely fastidious taste for mortifying the body, Lawrence looked disapprovingly at Abdullah, and noted that 'though only 35, he was putting on flesh'. He suspected him of insincerity, and of what he called 'a constant cheerfulness'. Abdullah, for his part, kept a wary eye on what he considered to be the motives behind Lawrence's questions, and hoped to keep a British officer from exerting any great influence on the Bedouin tribesmen of the interior of the peninsula.

The only candidate left for Lawrence, then, was Feisal – an unknown quantity in terms of personality, who was then in camp with 7,000 men more than 200 miles to the north, at Hamra, just inland from the coast. It took all Storrs' forceful diplomacy, and all the impression of competence which Lawrence had made on the watchful Abdullah, to get permission from Husein for Lawrence to visit Feisal in camp. The operation to obtain this safe-conduct was conducted on the telephone from Jeddah to Husein's headquarters in Mecca – the telephone being a fascinating innovation on which the Arabs at Jeddah occasionally listened to a captured Turkish brass band playing to Husein's instructions over the forty-five miles of line from Mecca. At last, a grudging permission was secured. Two days later, Lawrence sailed for the port of Rabegh a little to the north – 'to walk from that moment', as Storrs wrote later, 'into the pages of history . . .'

At Rabegh Lawrence met and talked

with Ali, whom he liked, but whose poor health confirmed his impression that this was not the man for the job. After sunset, so that the departure was secret from watching Bedouin eyes, Lawrence set out, with an escort of two trusted tribesmen, to ride north to meet Feisal. He wore an Arab cloak and headcloth over his uniform, and he rode on a camel saddled with Ali's personal equipment. Even this, so close to the coast, was no easy journey. Pounding across the dazzling white, sandy plain, Lawrence – no stranger to desert journeys – found himself forced to muffle his face in his headcloth, to protect his eyes from the glassy-glitter of the sun-beaten sand, from which the heat rose in rolling waves to sap and dry his body. He found a new food – the hand-crumbled dough cake of the Hedjaz, moistened with butter and sweetened with coarse sugar, which his companions pressed upon him. He records that he ate little – possibly setting the pattern for a future in which he would rival any Bedouin in terms of personal austerity. He had already noted that 'it was thought effeminate by the Arabs to carry a provision of food for a little journey of one hundred miles . . .' After two days, he reached Feisal.

The two men appear to have reached a swift understanding, though there is some later evidence that it was not quite so quick or so complete as Lawrence's own account in *Seven Pillars* would indicate. Feisal, then thirty-two years old, was a tall, slim man, wearing the white silk robes and the scarlet and gold headdress of an Arab prince, with a curved gold dagger in his belt. He greeted Lawrence with the slow, polite small-talk which is the invariable courtesy extended to a stranger in the Bedouin *mjalis*, or council tent. He spoke about Lawrence's journey, and remarked that he had ridden quickly for the time of year. On Lawrence's own account, Feisal then asked him conventionally: 'How do you like our place here in Wadi Safra?' Lawrence jumped in swiftly: 'Well, but it is far from Damascus.' There was a pause while Feisal twisted his dagger in his highly-strung nervous way. At last he smiled and said to Lawrence 'Praise be to God, there are Turks nearer to us than that.' For the moment, the interview was over.

The negotiations which followed cannot be understood unless it is clearly grasped that Feisal and Lawrence both sought different things – not only different things indeed, but things which were basically at odds with each other. Feisal was an Arab. He sought Arab independence. Paradoxically, however both he and Abdullah wanted to have British troops to help them secure this objective. Lawrence was British. He sought a better position for Britain in the Middle East as a lever against the Turks and, ultimately, the German enemy. Certainly, at this time, the idea of any sort of unqualified support for Arab independence is most unlikely to have entered his head. However, equally paradoxically he was strongly against the use of British or French troops to stiffen the Arab armies in the peninsula. He considered that a British landing would swing the Bedouin tribes against Husein. Instead, he believed that with technical assistance from a small number of British officers Feisal was militarily capable of doing the job for himself. He had spent some time walking through Feisal's positions, assessing the qualities of the tribesmen who sheltered in the shade of rocks and bushes in the hot *wadis*. He noted that they were superbly fit – 'physically thin, but exquisitely made, moving with an oiled activity altogether delightful to watch. It did not seem possible that men could be hardier or harder . . .' They were also in good spirits, happy at the chance of fighting, and even more so at the floods of money pouring in upon them. Husein was holding them in the field by paying £2 a month for a man and

Ronald Storrs, in 1916 Oriental Secretary to the British Agency in Egypt, whom Lawrence accompanied on a mission to Jedda in October of that year

£4 for a camel, plus a bonus of £1 a man for a prisoner.

Lawrence now returned to Jedah, where he found the 12,000-ton armoured cruiser *Euryalus,* and was given a passage back to Port Sudan, from where he went on to Khartoum and then to Cairo. He found that General Sir Reginald Wingate, Governor General of the Sudan, who also had overall control of British liaison with Husein, was of the opinion that British or Allied troops *were* needed to sustain the Arab Revolt. Wingate was also being supported by his French counterpart, Colonel Bremond, who urged the landing of Allied contingents in the Hedjaz for reasons, Lawrence believed, not unconnected with French territorial ambitions in Syria.

However, Lawrence now found himself unexpectedly popular with the staff in Cairo. General Sir Archibald Murray, who was commanding in Egypt, approved his views about reinforcements – or rather about no reinforcements – for Husein. Murray was a soldierly but cautious figure, and he was strongly averse to launching his forces into the relatively unknown Hedjaz on an unpredictable and open-ended campaign, with Bedouin allies whose loyalty was notoriously suspect, and whose stomach for a continued fight was by no means certain. In London, the Chief of the Imperial General Staff, Sir William Robertson, was in complete agreement with Murray – and thus with Lawrence. He strongly opposed Wingate's suggestions of an expeditionary force of a brigade with extra artillery. 'I could never,' he

warned the War Committee, 'bring myself to issue an order for British troops to be employed in the manner contemplated.' In the comfort of hindsight, we can see that Lawrence, Murray and Robertson were right, and that such an expedition, beginning with a brigade, would have swollen to divisions and almost certainly ended, eventually, in disaster. Lawrence never gave more important service to Britain than when he opposed the sending of British reinforcements to Husein.

In the meantime, however, he had also done service to himself by expressing sound views. At the end of the year, he was appointed liaison officer to Feisal's forces – partly, no doubt, as a reward for having told the staffs both in Cairo and in London exactly what they wanted to hear. Rather unexpectedly, he demurred for a moment. 'I was unlike a soldier: hated soldiering,' he wrote later. '. . . Of course, I had read the usual books . . . But I had never thought myself into the mind of a real commander compelled to fight a campaign of his own . . .' Lawrence was writing this after the war, of course. One wonders if, at the beginning of 1917, he had already inflated his future position as liaison officer and adviser to Feisal into 'a campaign of his own'.

Early in December 1917, Lawrence landed once more at Yenbo, a small port a little to the north of Feisal's previous position at Hamra. It was an unpropitious moment. The dark cloud of defeat hung heavy above the whole of the Arab revolt, and there must have been many moments when Lawrence felt that his presence in Arabia was rather in the nature of a spectator at a funeral than of an inspirer of victory. There had already been some Allied help further south, at Rabegh, where a flight of four BE biplanes had been established to counter Turkish aircraft; guns of various kinds – some of them, admittedly, obsolete by Western Front standards – were coming in; French

The Emir Feisal, selected from Husein's sons by Lawrence as the Arabs' war leader

General Sir Reginald Wingate
recommended British or Allied troop
support for the Arab rebellion in
opposition to Lawrence and others

Sir William Robertson, Chief of the
Imperial General Staff, agreed with
Lawrence; no British or Allied
reinforcements would be sent to Husein

gunner teams were promised; and a
handful of British officers and NCOs
were beginning to acquaint the
Bedouin with some of the simple
mysteries of technical warfare. It was
from one of these, the explosive
expert, Captain Garland, that Law
rence learned the technique of railway
demolition. There was a deep chord
in Lawrence which never failed to
respond to a really dedicated tech
nician and he admired Garland. He
was, he said, a man who was never at a
loss.

Yet in spite of this activity farther
south, at Yenbo the picture was
grim. Riding through the night to
Feisal's camp at Mubarak, a little
inland from Yenbo, Lawrence soon
discovered why. Feisal told him that
a Turkish force had outflanked his
outposts, attacked his brother Zeid's
positions further south (almost cap
turing Zeid asleep in his tent), and
were now moving on Yenbo. The night

scene in the date gardens of Mubarak was full of confused alarm: the whole area was dotted by hundreds of fires of thornwood, beside which weary tribesmen lay sleeping muffled in their cloaks, while around them the camels roared, and the bringers of bad tidings rode into camp to shout their latest rumour. However, the night passed without a Turkish assault, and with dawn came rational reflection and new hope.

The reflection came from Lawrence, but it was Feisal himself who rose to the occasion to supply the hope. It was difficult for Lawrence to arrive at any conclusion as to what the Turks – about whose strength there were wildly differing reports – might do: they might either strike straight for Yenbo, or simply bar Feisal's way south while the greater part of their force attacked Rabegh and Mecca. It seemed to Lawrence that perhaps the best thing that could happen

**British BE 2c biplanes, brought in to counter the Turkish airforce**

was that the Turks should be lured to waste time trying to deal with the 5,000 men with Feisal at Mubarak, which would give the Arabs time to prepare Yenbo for an assault. Meanwhile, all Lawrence could do was to wait and watch how Feisal would set about restoring the uneasy morale of his tribal force.

The next forty-eight hours convinced him that he had been right in backing Feisal's claim to lead the Revolt. Next morning Feisal moved his positions, partly for tactical considerations, but mainly for the sound psychological reason of giving his men something to occupy their volatile and anxious minds. That was a first, clear indication of Feisal's quality as a leader, but there was much more to come. In the next few hours, Lawrence, watching Feisal,

Feisal (in light coloured clothing) with a bodyguard of Ageyl tribesmen. His handling of his tribal sheiks made a favourable impression on Lawrence

realised that he was observing a master handler of Bedouin tribesmen.

Feisal listened to all complaints and all fears, with phenomenal patience and quiet humour. When the sheiks of the Harb and Ageyl tribes, whose foolishness at the outposts had precipitated the situation, came to Feisal for audience, Lawrence had grimly anticipated an explosion of wrathful reproach. This did not happen: instead, there was chaff and joking and tact – and not the public humiliation which no Bedouin could stomach. 'I never,' Lawrence wrote later, 'saw an Arab leave him dissatisfied or hurt . . .'

Meanwhile, the Turks did not attack. There were five British warships in the harbour at Yenbo, including the 540-ton shallow draught monitor M31, whose twin 6-inch guns dominated the likely Turkish approach. The warships' searchlights flooded the shore line and the plain above it, and the prospect of attacking under the very muzzles of these powerful mobile batteries and the electric glare of their equipment was probably the deciding factor which constrained the Turks to withdraw into the hills, content with a very limited success. Lawrence's own view of this fatal hesitation was that it cost the Turks the campaign.

Lawrence was now settling into the new pattern of military life which he found at Fiesal's headquarters. At daybreak, the Imam called everyone to prayer. This was followed by a dawn cup of coffee, and then a visit to Feisal's tent, to hear the news of the night. Then a tray of breakfast dates with possibly a spiced cake from Feisal's grandmother in Mecca, then more coffee and sweet tea. During the morning, Feisal listened to suppliants and complainers. Lunch was simple tray of spinach, lentils, rice, beans and cakes. Like Lawrence, Feisal was a fastidious, small eater. Those sheiks in his retinue with larger appetites were compelled to stave off hunger by ordering a second, bigger lunch when they returned to the privacy of their own tents. In the afternoon, Feisal would walk round his positions, and in the evening there was the planning of patrols and future activity. The evening meal was much like lunch, but contained the greatest amount of protein of the day – lumps of boiled mutton bedded on rice.

After a few days, Feisal asked Lawrence to wear Arab clothes instead of his British Khaki. It would, he said, prevent him from being mistaken for a Turkish officer, and would mean that he would be far less conspicuous to inquisitive Bedouin eyes when he entered or left the council tent. Nothing could have suited Lawrence better. He was usually both unhappy and untidy in British uniform, and he had already decided that there were sound psychological as well as physical reasons for adopting the dress of those with whom he lived and beside whom he must soon fight. He gave his reasoning in a series of rules for British liaison officers, written soon after joining Feisal, which he called *The Twenty Seven Articles*. This confidential set of instructions gives a clear picture of how Lawrence learned to work with an alien people, and how sharp and effective his mind was when in came to getting his own way with them. There can be no doubt that some of these 'articles' were the direct result of watching Feisal at work.

'Handling Hejaz Arabs,' he wrote, 'is an art, not a science . . .' Of the

**The monitor *M31* was one of five British warships whose presence discouraged Turkish attack on the harbour town of Yenbo**

twenty-seven rules which followed this opening statement, some are little more than ordinary precepts of leadership, but others reveal a deep psychological insight into the Arab mentality. On the Bedouin themselves: 'Learn all you can about your Sherifs and Bedu. Get to know their families, clans and tribes, friends and enemies, wells, hills, and roads. Do all this by listening and by indirect inquiry. Do not ask questions. Get to speak their dialect of Arabic, not yours. Until you can understand their allusions, avoid getting deep into conversation, or you will drop bricks.'

On fighting: 'Do not try to trade on what you know on fighting. The Hejaz confounds ordinary tactics. Learn the Bedu principles of war as thoroughly and as quickly as you can, for till you know them your advice will be no good to the Sherif. Unnumbered generations of tribal raids have taught them more about some parts of the business than we shall ever know. In familiar conditions they fight well, but strange events cause panics. Keep your unit small.'

On how to handle an Arab commander: 'Win and keep the confidence of your leader. Strengthen his prestige at your expense before others if you can. Never refuse or quash schemes he may put forward, but ensure that they are put forward in the first instance privately to you. Always approve them, and after praise modify them insensibly, causing the suggestions to come from him, until they are in accord with your own opinion. When you attain this point hold him to it, keep a tight grip of his ideas, and push him forward as firmly as possible, but secretly, so that no one but himself (and he not too clearly) is aware of your pressure.'

On wearing Arab clothes: '. . . If you can wear Arab kit when with the tribes you will acquire their trust and intimacy to a degree impossible in uniform. It is, however, dangerous and difficult. They make no special

allowances for you when you dress like them. You will be like an actor in a foreign theatre, playing a part day and night for months, without rest, and for an anxious stake . . . If you wear Arab things at all, go the whole way. Leave your English friends and customs on the coast, and fall back on Arab habits entirely. It is possible, starting thus level with them, for the European to beat the Arabs at their own game, for we have stronger motives for our action, and put more heart into it than they. If you can surpass them, you have taken an immense stride towards complete success, but the strain of living and thinking in a foreign and half-understood language, the savage food, strange clothes, and stranger ways, with the complete loss of privacy and quiet, and the impossibility of ever relaxing your watchful imitation of others for months on end, provide such an added stress to the ordinary difficulties of dealing with the Bedu, the climate, and the Turk that this road should not be chosen without serious thought . . .'

After reading that paragraph, one can, for a moment, glimpse what the years ahead would cost Lawrence, and the efforts he would have to make to adapt himself for his role. He summed up the daunting nature of his task in his last, twenty-seventh article:

'The beginning and the end of handling Arabs is unremitting study of them. Keep always on your guard; never say an unnecessary thing: Watch yourself, and your companions all the time: Hear all that passes, search out what is going on beneath the surface, read their characters, discover their tastes and weaknesses, and keep everything you find out to yourself . . . Your success will be proportioned to the amount of mental effort you devote to it . . .'

# Shape of a campaign

Lawrence could not spend long in learning how to handle Feisal, or even in becoming familiar with the military routine of the camp. Arab armies are not, in general, good at standing still, and Feisal's was no exception. After the alarms of the recent past, something was needed to bind men more closely to the cause of the Revolt, and to its leader. Foremost in Lawrence's mind at this time – and indeed in most British military minds concerned with the Arab Revolt – was the capture of Medina, which was regarded as an indispensable preliminary to any further large-scale military move. Lawrence now went down to Rabegh to discuss plans with another British senior military adviser, Colonel Wilson. He also found there the French Colonel Bremond – described in *Seven Pillars*, not without a delicate irony, as 'the only real soldier in Hejaz'.

The key factor of the strategic situation was the 850-mile line of the Hejaz railway, running down from Damascus, through Amman and Ma'an to Medina. While this remained intact, the Turks could supply Medina and threaten Mecca. Still with the capture of Medina uppermost in his mind, Lawrence – firmly backed by Wilson – wished to persuade Feisal to revive an earlier Arab plan to move north from Yenbo and seize the port of Wejh. This would then become a base and supply depot from which Bedouin columns might raid out into the desert and cut the line well north of the Turks in the beleaguered city.

At once, there was a clash with Bremond. The Frenchman also wanted to capture Medina, but he wanted to achieve this with an Allied – i.e. British and French – force. The Sykes-Picot agreement between Britain and France in the previous year had planned to divide the Ottoman Empire between Britain, France and Russia. Roughly speaking, France had been given the predominant say in the area of what is now Lebanon and Syria west of Aleppo, Homs, and Damascus, and Britain a similar status in the territory between Bagdad and the port of Basra on the Persian Gulf. The vast area between these two spheres of influence was to become an independent

A charge explodes in the campaign of sabotage directed at the Hejaz railway

Arab state. Thus any military movement of Arab forces north towards Syria was seen by Bremond as a possible complicating factor for French ambitions in the area after ultimate victory had been achieved. In any case, Bremond had a poor opinion of the plan from a practical point of view. He did not believe that these 'savages', as he called the Arabs, could capture Wejh. Such an idea, he remarked gloomily to Lawrence, was 'military suicide'.

Lawrence and Wilson, on the other hand, were quite certain that the capture of Wejh was within Arab powers, provided Feisal's forces received the artillery support of the Royal Navy along the coast. Feisal, too, had been worried about the risks, but he was soon won over by the urging of the British officers. The plan went ahead, and – according to Bremond – its details were kept secret from the French.

Meanwhile, on 2nd January 1917, Lawrence had a first, experimental taste of Bedouin warfare. He rode out with a handful of camel-raiders to a point overlooking a Turkish position, opened fire on the tents and withdrew. It was hardly a glittering action, but it may have taught him a lesson or two about Bedouin mobility. Lawrence's Arab biographer, Suleiman Mousa, remarks disapprovingly that 'this was Lawrence's first participation in a military operation – even a minor skirmish – and this was a full seven months after the outbreak of the Arab Revolt . . .' Since Lawrence had only been appointed to serve in Arabia in the previous month, the tone of disapproval seems somewhat harsh.

On the day following this little raid, 3rd January, Feisal marched on Wejh with a force of 10,000 men. It was a scene very different from those of the war being fought thousands of miles away on the Western Front. It

**Feisal at the head of his troops nearing Yenbo**

Colonel Wilson (in sun helmet) and his staff. He met Lawrence at Rabegh to discuss tactics

was, said Lawrence, splendid and barbaric – a column of glittering, gaily-coloured tribesmen, hundreds of camels, the Bedouin singing their *extempore* ballads in their high, tuneless voices, the whole panoply of an Arab army on the march. Lawrence was joined by two Englishmen on the way to Wejh. The first was a gunner officer, Vickery, whom he detested, and who disliked him quite as heartily. Vickery though Lawrence a militarily incompetent fool and a braggart, while Lawrence – possibly somewhat jealous of the fact that Vickery's spoken Arabic was very much better than his own – saw Vickery as an unimaginative professional soldier who lacked fire and vision. However, Vickery soon left the land expedition to join a naval party, which was carrying several hundred tribal irregulars as an auxiliary landing force. The second Englishman was much more welcome – the Newcombe with whom Lawrence

had conducted his map survey c Sinai just before the outbreak c war. Newcombe was now a lieutenan colonel, and thus technically senio to Lawrence. However, he shared th same views as Lawrence, and the tw found no difficulty in working tc gether, irrespective of nominal rank then or at any other time.

The march to Wejh hardly turne out to be a model operation. The firs half of the 200-mile trek went we enough, but after that the planne advance went hopelessly awry. Th country was bleak and inhospitabl even by desert standards. Newcomb rode ahead of the exhausted force and managed to get them supplie from one of the supporting nava ships at Habban, to the south o Wejh. As they ate and drank, th hungry, thirsty tribesmen hear gunfire to the north. The naval party unable to wait longer, had landed it. Arab auxiliaries and captured th town. Feisal's army straggled in ove the next three days. Lawrence wa even more ill-pleased when he dis covered that the landing operatio had been directed by the triumphan

ickery, with a loss of only twenty
~~dead~~. The two had a bitter wrangle,
in which Lawrence maintained that
even twenty dead was too high a
figure, since the Turks would have
been forced to surrender bloodlessly
in a few days. It was not a reassuring
beginning to Lawrence's mission with
Feisal.

For the Turks, however, the loss of
Wejh was a most alarming event, and
Fakhri Pasha pulled back his forces
to cover Medina. The Hejaz railway
was about 150 miles to the east, but
the initiative now lay with Feisal.
Fakhri Pasha established some forces
to try to cover the railway line north
of Medina. Two main bodies were
formed – the so-called Second Composite Force of 5,000 men based at
Tebuk, 300 miles up the line from
Medina, and the First Composite
Force much farther north at Ma'an.
This numbered about 7,000 men, and
included some battalions of the Tur-
ish Seventh Division withdrawn
for this purpose from Syria. However,
these forces were not held as strategic
groups, since the Bedouin rarely put
themselves in a position in which

they would be vulnerable to strategic
attack. Instead, the Turkish command was forced to parcel out its
forces in camps and garrisons along
the line, offering excellent targets
for Bedouin raids. The Turks, in fact,
had moved to the defensive – never a
good military posture from which to
counter guerillas.

A few days after the capture of
Wejh, Lawrence paid a quick visit to
Cairo. His stock, and that of the
Arabs, was high there now that a
dividend had been shown. Even the
implacable Bremond called to see
him with his congratulations – and
with a new plan for capturing Aqaba,
the only Turkish-controlled port left
on the Red Sea. He wanted this to be
carried out by an Anglo-French force.
Lawrence suspected, probably correctly, Bremond's intention was to
confine Arab military activity to the
interior of the Hejaz effectively stabi-

53

'... the greatest fighting man in north Arabia'; Lawrence's description of Auda abu Tayi

lising it round Medina. Lawrence had his own plans for Aqaba, but they did not include an Anglo-French force. Hurrying back to Wejh, he succeeded in forestalling Bremond who had himself gone there to put his proposal to Feisal.

The Revolt was now gaining both equipment and adherents. A great deal in the way of military stores was being landed at Wejh – machine guns, rifles, a radio station, even a couple of Rolls Royce armoured cars released from the East Africa campaign, crewed by British soldiers from the Army Service Corps and the Machine Gun Corps. But the camp was widely dispersed and the Bedouin were bored: Lawrence spent some of the time in deliberately walking barefoot over the hot ground, in an attempt further to harden his body for the trials

ahead. Meanwhile, a group of Bedoui found an old seaplane bomb lying i the town, detonated it, and blev themselves to bits, scattering blood arms and legs among the tents.

It was at this point that the legend ary Auda abu Tayi, whom Lawrenc described as 'the greatest fightin man in north Arabia' arrived a Feisal's side. Auda, the principa sheik of the Howeitat tribe, was story-book figure who appears t have stepped straight from a dese romance. The portrait by Eric Ker nington in *Seven Pillars* tells a goo deal about him at a glance – a stron cruel, but strangely sensitive fac proud fierce eyes, an indefinable air command. He was now more tha fifty years old, his black hair streake with white. He had killed seventy-fiv Bedouin in battle and tribal raid probably more Turks, though he di dained to list them. He had bee wounded thirteen times – and marri twenty-eight times. His presenc eside Feisal was essential if the ribes between Ma'an and Aqaba ere to allow Feisal unhampered assage, or join him on his long rusade to the north. For it was to the orth that Lawrence's thoughts had ow turned, away from Medina and ae problem of capturing it. To see hy this happened, we must go back little in time.

Soon after the capture of Wejh, ae Egyptian patrol vessel *Nur el ahr* brought to Lawrence an inter-epted telegram from the Turkish ommander Jemal Pasha to Fakhri asha in Medina. This appeared to rder the instant abandonment of Iedina, and the moving of its garrison orth to reinforce the Turkish front ;ainst the British in Palestine. lthough this seemed at first sight ) be what both Arabs and Allies anted, it did not suit the British ommander, Sir Archibald Murray, ho feared the effect of Turkish rein-rcements further north. Murray ow wanted the Arabs either to

storm Medina and thus eliminate the Turkish garrison before it could break out, or at least to neutralise the Turks inside the city by effec-tively blowing up the Hejaz railway line. Feisal and Lawrence agreed with these proposals, and on 10th March 1917, Lawrence set out on a 125-mile camel ride through the mountains south of Wejh to reach Abdullah's positions to warn him to be ready to attack the Turks if they decided to leave Medina.

It was a nightmare journey. Lawrence was already ill with dysen-tery when he left Wejh, and his back was covered with painful boils. The jolting of the camel and the fierce heat in the valleys of black lava brought on fever and blinding head-ache; the Bedouin escort quarrelled amongst themselves; and then, as

**The Turkish commander Jemal Pasha, whose directive ordering the Medina garrison north to Palestine was intercepted and brought to Lawrence**

Lawrence's military studies included the works of, left to right: Clausewitz, Moltke, Napoleon and Marshal Saxe

they crossed the rocky Wadi Kiten, a shot was fired. A Moorish soldier had killed a tribesman of the Ageyl during a bitter dispute. The Ageyl, firm on custom, demanded blood for blood. Staring at their grim, angry faces through aching eyes, Lawrence realised with a sinking heart that blood for blood might well continue, with other Moroccans claiming blood for the blood which had been exacted from them. There was one possible solution. Lawrence drew his revolver, and motioned the Moroccan into a gully, where he shot him. The Moroccan died horribly, crying and shrieking during each of the three shots it took to kill him. 'At least,' Lawrence wrote bitterly, 'no revenge could lie against my followers, for I was a stranger and kinless . . .' Three days later, he reached Abdullah's camp at Abu Markha, delivered his message, and collapsed.

He spent the next ten days, partly in high fever, partly in convalescence, lying in a tent in Abdullah's camp. Possibly as a means of escape from the memories of his traumatic journey, and the dreadful death of the Moroccan, he forced his mind to re examine the purposes of the Ara campaign, and his own purpose i being there. They were the most in portant ten days of his life: h glittering fame and his considerabl influence on events date from the r flections and the decisions of thos uncomfortable hours, sweating, irr tated by flies, listening to the bellow ing roar of the camels outside.

He began by examining the abstrac classical theories of war which ha interested him in the early days. we accept Lawrence's own accou of the reading he had done on war, must be admitted that it was pr digious, either for a professional an amateur. He told Sir Basil Lidde Hart after the war that he had beg with 'schoolboy stuff' – Creasy Decisive Battles, Mahan's Influence Sea Power upon History, Henderson Stonewall Jackson, Coxe's Marlboroug From there he had gone on to Claus witz and Moltke, to the Prussia staff officer von der Goltz, to Foch a eventually back to Napoleon. between these magisterial works, had 'browsed' through the thirty-tv volumes of Napoleon's correspon ence, and also examined castle buil ing and siege operations in the pag of Procopius, Vegetius, and Polic cetes. After studying the Napoleon

stem, he had gone back further
ill, to the master of war whom
apoleon himself had studied, the
th Century Marshal Saxe. He had
so conducted more practical studies
visiting and examining the battle-
lds of Rocroi, Crecy, Agincourt,
alplaquet, Sedan, and going to the
ea of Valmy, trying 'to re-fight the
1ole of Marlborough's wars'.
Admittedly Lawrence was one of the
w human beings of any age whose
ind sometimes touched the level of
nius. Nevertheless, it is not possible
accept these assertions at face
lue. The programme of study which
awrence said he followed in his
are time would have taken an
telligent professional many years:
equately to examine Mahan, Hen-
rson, and Napier alone is a daunting
ademic task. To say this is not, of
urse, to dismiss Lawrence's reading
war, nor its influence on him. He
.s an omnivorous and quick reader,
d he undoubtedly cast his eye over
1ch of what he claimed to have
1died. It is the depth rather than
e scope of his reading which is
en to doubt. Both before and after
is time, Lawrence displayed one
tstanding intellectual character-
ic. He had a devastating intuition,
out people and about war. Like
ny intellectuals, this intuition did

not satisfy him as a source of decision,
and he was constantly at pains – with
those whom he wished to impress – to
support it by apparently solid
reasoning.

It is in this after-the-event intellectual justification of decisions taken
correctly but intuitively that one
can see the basis of the charges of
exaggeration and even falsehood
which were made against Lawrence
in later years.

Nevertheless, lying in Abdullah's
camp, Lawrence did review what he
knew about war, and he did arrive at
certain conclusions. The most sig-
nificant of these was that the capture
of Medina was not important – and
that it might even be counter-
productive to the Arab effort. As he
lay thinking, fanning the flies from
his sweating face, he saw clearly – so
he tells us – that Medina was not
needed as a base from which the
Arabs could work, was not a threat
now that they already held Wejh, and
was to the Turks merely an encum-
brance which bottled up useful troops,
and ate up supplies. Medina, in fact,
was more useful to the Revolt in
Turkish hands than in Arab. The
Arabs had already won the Hejaz
war, since Feisal's aim was geo-
graphical, and less than one per cent
of the Hejaz was now under effective

ccording to Sir Basil Liddell Hart
wrence's ' . . . theoretical mastery of
ar . . . was unique'

urkish control.

Lawrence now arrived at a further nclusion – that the way to maintain d extend this victory was not by nventional battle. The Bedouin, he ew, would not accept casualties on ything like a proportionate estern Front scale. Mass killing s completely alien to their tribal adition and fighting practice. In y case, in pitched battle the edouin lost their decisive advantage mobility, and threw themselves ainst the Turkish advantage of trenched fire-power. The Arabs re not an army, as Napoleon, ausewitz, and Foch understood the rld. 'Armies,' thought Lawrence, ere like plants, immobile, firm-oted, nourished through long stems the head. We might be a vapour, owing where we listed . . . It seemed regular soldier might be helpless thout a target . . .' Thus it was the oidance of pitched battle, on the eories of Marshal Saxe, rather than ecisive' confrontation, on the eories of Napoleon, that Lawrence w decided to make the *leitmotif* of e Arab Revolt. It was, in essence, e strategy of indirect approach, ich in another context was to be eached so fervently by the British eorist, Sir Basil Liddell Hart after 18.

t was on this reasoning that Liddell rt felt that Lawrence should be mitted to the company of the Great ptains of history. The Liddell rt verdict was that Lawrence ex-bited 'a theoretical mastery of war at was unique. His personality nsmitted this into a practical stery . . . He not only earns a place ong the masters of war, but stands t among them by the clearness of understanding of his art . . .' wrence's military reveries, how-er, have been dismissed as etentious' by some commentators,

and by the Arab historian Suleiman Mousa as 'no more than ink on paper'.

Before any assessment can be made, there is one vital question to be answered. How far could the tactics or strategy of the campaign be personally affected by Lawrence? His own words were: 'I was unfortunately as much in command of the campaign as I pleased, and was untrained . . .' At face value, the words seem to convey an absurdly inflated image of Lawrence's real role. Here was a young staff-captain, former don, former archaeologist, quite unversed in the practicalities of warfare, asserting that he was able to control the strategy and movements of tens of thousands of fighting men, of a proud, suspicious and alien race. To do this, of course, he must effectively dominate their leader, Feisal. If, indeed, Lawrence was in effect commander-in-chief of the Arab force, what was he doing far away from it, lying in a tent in Abdullah's camp? According to disenchanted com-mentators of later years, the whole thing was one more example of Lawrence's talent for magnifying his role, and one cannot help but feel some sympathy for this view. Yet reflection shows that this cannot have been the whole truth, Lawrence's own *Twenty-Seven Articles* – a model for any aspiring liaison officer – reveal just how he went about getting his own way, and there is no reason to believe that he was unsuccessful with Feisal. The history of the next few months would show that the Revolt did, on the whole, develop the way Lawrence wanted. And there is clear evidence that in Cairo, British generals – some of them, like Allenby, of the highest intelligence and pro-fessional ability – believed that they were, in a sense, dealing with another commander-in-chief when they dealt with Lawrence. Lawrence's own words probably provide the clue: 'I was as much in command of the campaign as I pleased . . .' In other words, his position with Feisal was such that he

59

**Captain Raho, who had made successful raids with Colonel Newcombe, joined Lawrence on his first railway sabotage mission**

could persuade the Arab leader
follow any course of action which b
Lawrence, desired. He was n
commander-in-chief – but his positio
gave him virtually the same influen
on events.

As Lawrence recovered from h
sickness, he began to speak
Abdullah about his future. He foun
once more, that Abdullah irritat
him. He was talkative but lethargi
always ready to discuss the wid
social world of Europe, or the dista
Battle of the Somme, but annoying
indifferent to immediate plans. In o
sense, of course, this inactivity suit
Lawrence's new mood, for Abdull
was most unlikely to make a front
assault on Medina. Lawrence n
reasoned that a series of pin-pri
attacks on the Hejaz railway wou
inhibit the Turks from trying
evacuate the city – a break-out whi
might provoke the pitched battle
feared. On 26th March, Lawrence s
out to make a demonstration raid f
Abdullah. This was Lawrence's fi
attack on the railway, but it was n
by any means the first attack that h
been carried out. The efficient a
gallant Garland; who had taught h
technique to Lawrence, blew up t
first train on 20th February about
miles up the line from Medina, a
over the ensuing weeks both t
French captaine Raho and Color
Newcombe had made effective raids

It was, indeed, Raho – an Arab
speaking officer from French Nor
Africa – who accompanied Lawren
on his raid from Abdullah's camp. T
operation was no more than a qualifi
success – only about half the promis
Arab force arrived at the rendezvo
so that the railway station at Aba
Naam, which Lawrence chose
target, could not be stormed as he h
hoped. However, they did damage t
station and an engine as well
cutting the line and bringing ba
thirty prisoners from the 400-stro
Turkish garrison. It was a poin
for the future.

When he returned to Feisal at We

erif Nasir of Medina was a member of
wrence's pre-Aqaba mission raiding
d recruiting party

it was mid-April, and Auda was there in person to confirm his allegiance to the Arab cause. The old warrior proved his good faith in a comic way: at the ceremonial banquet to mark his arrival, he suddenly rushed from the tent, tore his false teeth from his mouth, and pounded them to pieces with a stone. 'I had forgotten,' he explained, between blows. 'Jemal Pasha (the Turkish commander) gave me these. I was eating my lord's bread with Turkish teeth...'

Lawrence's task now was to try to convince his British colleagues that the changed strategy he had evolved in Abdullah's sick-tent was the right one to adopt. He talked it over with them – with Colonel Joyce, the senior British adviser to Husein; with Garland, busy with arranging new raids; with Newcombe, planning to capture a whole stretch of the line. Lawrence put forward his proposition that to try to capture Medina, or even permanently to interrupt the railway line, would lead to a battle which the Arabs could not win. Instead, Lawrence wanted to capture the northern port of Aqaba – not from the sea, as Wejh had been captured, but by a raid from the eastward hinterland behind the port. The British officers listened, only half-convinced, and already deeply involved in their own military affairs. The best that Lawrence could achieve with them was 'a qualified admission' that his plan to take Aqaba might, at least, be useful in taking Turkish attention away from their projected operations around Medina.

Arab historians have ascribed the birth of the Aqaba plan both to Feisal and to Auda, from whom, they assert, Lawrence merely adopted it. It is quite impossible now to decide if this was so – and in any case, the point is hardly worth the argument that has been devoted to it. Whoever first thought of the plan, all three

certainly supported it. For Feisal, i offered another, big step to the north and a wider stage. Lawrence himsel; as will be seen, was becoming increasingly intellectually bound u; with the Arab motivation of th Revolt – and in any case, from ; purely British standpoint, the occupa tion of Aqaba would assist Ara: forces in Palestine and Syria t support the slowly-moving Britis: offensive from Sinai. In this matter all three were of one mind. Lawrenc

**The party supplemented their diet with desert game, such as this oryx**

decided not to wait for orders, but wrote to Colonel Clayton, the Intelligence chief in the Middle East, and informed him of what he was about to do. Then, on 9th May, he set out north with a small scouting party of about forty picked camelry, travelling light. Each man had with him a 45-lb bag of flour, and the baggage camels carried six camel-loads of explosive and £20,000 in gold. Beside him rode Auda himself, and Auda's cousin, the Sherif Nasir of Medina. Moving across

a weird, arid landscape, they took eleven days to reach the Hejaz railway at Dizad, south of Tebuk. As they passed, they blew the line, much to Auda's delight, and pushed on, living on gazelle and an occasional oryx, until they reached the tents of the Howeitat tribe in the Wadi Sirhan. It was nineteen days since they had left Wejh, and Lawrence had proved one thing. He could ride and endure with any Bedouin.

Auda, Nasir and the others were now

busy recruiting the Howeitat to Feisal's side, building a force for the descent upon Aqaba. It was work in which Lawrence could play little part, and his mind now turned to a new adventure - nothing less than a long ride behind the enemy lines, north to Syria and Damascus. Of all Lawrence's exploits in Arabia, this ride was the most controversial, and the episode on which most doubt has been thrown by his critics.

It is true that in *Seven Pillars*, Lawrence is extraordinarily vague about this trip. 'A rash adventure,' he called it, '(which) suited my abandoned mood . . .' Then follow a couple of pages of anxious reflection about the unsatisfactory nature of his position, sandwiched between Arab aspirations and British intentions, and of his decision to see to it that the Arab Revolt should be a success in its own Arab terms, as well as 'handmaiden to our Egyptian campaign'. He added: 'Therefore I undertook this long dangerous ride, in which to see the more important of Feisal's secret friends, and to study key-positions of our future campaigns . . .' Two paragraphs later, he begins: 'When I returned it was June the sixteenth . . .' What happened on this daring journey? There is hardly a word about it in *Seven Pillars*, nor afterwards did Lawrence ever reveal any detail about this exploit, going so far as to write to his biographer, Robert Graves, after the war:

'You may make public, if you like, that my reticence upon this northward raid is deliberate, and based on private reasons: and record your opinion that I have found mystification, and perhaps statements deliberately misleading or contradictory, the best way to hide the truth of what really occurred, if anything did occur...'

It was mysterious obfuscation of this kind, and certain discrepancies in dates, which made some critics conclude that the entire trip was a figment of Lawrence's over-active

## On Lawrence's extraordinary mission to Damascus he interviewed the Turkish commandant of the city, Ali Riza Pasha

imagination. It is, however, almost impossible to accept this view. First of all, Lawrence sent a report about the trip to the Arab Bureau and his chief Clayton, dated 10th July, 1917. The rough gist of this was that he had travelled alone, accompanied only by successive local guides, and had reached Damascus, where he had actually interviewed the Turkish base commandant of the city, Ali Riza Pasha - who, in spite of his position, had some contact with the underground currents of the Arab Revolt. He had also made an assessment of tribal loyalties in various parts of Syria - and incidentally blown up a small bridge near Raas Baalbeck. To send such a report, on such an important subject, to military intelligence in Cairo, would - if the report were untrue - be a totally irresponsible, foolish, even insane act. Lawrence was not irresponsible, foolish or insane.

The second important piece of evidence that the trip took place, and that its details were known and checked by his superiors, was that Wingate recommended Lawrence for the Victoria Cross for making it. Recommendations for the Victoria Cross are not casual affairs: this one, in fact, failed on the technical ground that it had not been witnessed by an officer. However, no recommendation could or would have been made on Lawrence's claim alone. There must have been completely convincing proof to highly qualified experts like Clayton that the trip took place. In fact, not long afterwards Lawrence was promoted major and made Companion of the Order of the Bath. A CB is an almost unheard-of honour for such a junior officer. Lawrence's reasons, however, for clouding the whole issue of his ride north remain an enigma to this day.

# The first victory: Aqaba

By mid-June 1917, when Lawrence returned to the Wadi Sirhan, old Auda had raised a force to take Aqaba. This consisted of about 500 picked men, camel-mounted. It was important to deceive the Turks as to the direction of the attack: during his mysterious ride Lawrence had dropped false hints of an impending Arab attack towards Damascus. However, he now decided to make a more concrete deception by raiding to the north against the railway between Amman and Deraa. The Aqaba expedition set off on 9th June, and Lawrence detached a hundred men and took them on a rapid march of about a hundred miles. They blew the line north of the Dhuleil bridge, and watched a party of Turkish soldiers with mules heading unknowningly along the line towards them. The Bedouin, hungry for mules, wanted to charge the Turks, counting on surprise to offset their lack of numbers. Lawrence asked Auda's nephew, Zaal, what he thought would be the Bedouin casualties if they *did* charge, Zaal guessed at five or six. Lawrence at once decided not to charge, in spite

of the furious protests of t[?] Howeitat. It was a good example [?] his tactical reasoning. His objecti[?] was Aqaba. Even half a dozen usef[?] men were too high a price for [?] unnecessary skirmish. It also in[?] cated another interesting factor in t[?] situation. The Bedouin, althoug[?] eager to fight, and led by a bloo[?] relative of the great Auda himse[?] did not charge. Lawrence was[?] effective command.

However, the Bedouin managed [?] shed some blood and get some loo[?] after all. Riding south, they sight[?] Atwi station, down the line fro[?] Amman. It was only a small post, a[?] it gave the Howeitat a chance for t[?] sort of action at which they excelle[?] They lined up behind the ridge abo[?] the line, and watched as Turki[?] officers and officials sipped coffe[?] sitting in the shade of the ticket offic[?] A Bedouin marksman picked off t[?] fattest of the officers, and then t[?] rest of the Howeitat poured in the[?] volleys until all the Turks lay dead [?] dying. Four soldiers coming down t[?]

**Descent on Aqaba**

line on a trolley were also killed.
The Bedouin looted everything they
could find, finishing by setting fire to
the wooden buildings. It was a classic
little pin-prick action of the kind
which was second nature to an Arab
tribesman, and infuriating and humi-
liating to the Turks.

A bigger action was soon to follow,
not long after Lawrence's detachment
rejoined Auda's main party. Not
completely deceived by the feints
towards the north, the Turks had
taken the precaution of blowing some
of the wells along Auda's route. In an
effort to forestall more Turkish
activity of this kind, the Arabs sent a
scouting party in advance to capture
and hold the important well at Aba
el Lissan, a little to the south-west of
Ma'an, and near which the Arab force
intended to hook round to the rear of

Aqaba. A skirmish at a Turkish post
alerted the Turks to the presence of
Auda's force, and as soon as the
main body arrived, it found itself
confronted by a Turkish infantry
battalion, additionally equipped with
mountain guns. This had now dug
itself in round the vital spring. The
Bedouin were going to have to fight
a battle.

They began in their traditional way,
creeping into position in the bowl of
hills which surrounded the little
valley of Aba el Lissan, and sniping
through the long hot day at the
Turkish infantry, hoping to goad them
out of their positions into a useless
and expensive charge. The Turks
stayed put, occasionally sending a
shell from a mountain gun to burst
pointlessly far behind the Bedouin
positions. Both sides were suffering
terribly under the heat hammer of the
Arabian noon. The end to this ordeal
came suddenly when Auda himself,
furious at Lawrence's scornful remark
that the Howeitat 'shoot a lot and hit

69

little,' charged fifty horsemen against the Turkish position, supported by Nasir's 400 camel riders, and broke it. Lawrence, on his racing camel Naama, rode down with Nasir in this wild charge, firing his pistol across her head. Suddenly Naama went down, flinging Lawrence many feet in front of her. One of Lawrence's hurried pistol shots from her heaving back had torn out the back of her skull. When Lawrence recovered consciousness, the last desperate remnants of the Turkish battalion were being butchered in the valley. Three hundred Turks lay dead or dying round the well. There were 160 Turkish prisoners. Bedouin casualties were astonishingly light. Two had been killed: 'it was, of course, a pity,' Lawrence wrote later, 'to lose any of our men . . .' Only the mountain guns and a few horsed officers escaped, fleeing up the road to Ma'an. Auda swaggered up to Lawrence, the marks of seven bullets in his clothes, but not a scratch on his skin. It was all stuff for another Bedouin ballad – though the Bedouin themselves were now at the more practical task of stripping the dead, marching off next morning wearing oddments of the uniforms of this annihilated Turkish infantry battalion.

At Auda's insistence, they moved in the night after the battle, since the old warrior feared that other rival tribes might take advantage of the weariness of Lawrence's force to snatch the abundant loot – mostly rifles and clothes – which it had gathered. First, however, Lawrence went down into the valley and walked among the stripped, ivory-hued corpses of the Turks, straightening the crumpled bodies, putting them all in order, one by one', as he wrote later. It was a curious little episode, and one which might have been of interest to a modern psychological investigator able to ask Lawrence further questions.

However, Lawrence was soon moved by more normal martial considerations. It was learned from the prisoners that Ma'an itself was garrisoned now by only two Turkish companies, which would be quite inadequate as a defence against the Arab force. The Howeitat were eager to turn aside and seize this Turkish depot, with all the plunder that such a capture would bring. Lawrence opposed this scheme, and brought both Auda and Nasir to his opinion. Aqaba was the objective: Aqaba was the heart of the strategy, and no tactical mirage such as that offered by Ma'an should deflect the Arabs from their original aim. He won the day. Slowly the Arab column wound on into the hills behind Aqaba, joined increasingly by loot-hungry tribesmen, while the Turkish officer prisoners complained bitterly about the poor quality of Arab rations.

Aqaba fell on 6th July, almost as an anticlimax, taken by surprise from its rearward defences. These were not strong, since the Turks had always imagined that the assault would be made, as in the case of Wejh, from the sea. There was only a brief period of parley with the Turkish garrison before – realising that there would be no reinforcement from Maan or the north – the Turks surrendered. The garrison of Aqaba brought the total of Turkish prisoners in the Arab's hands to 700. The town was empty, shattered by successive naval bombardments, short of food for tribesmen and Turks alike. Rations, arms and money were urgently needed. There was no wireless, which meant that Lawrence must himself return to Egypt to explain the position and get help. He set out by camel across the Sinai, reaching Suez in fifty hours – a remarkable march of 150 miles, stopping once at Themed for water.

From Suez, after a certain amount of bureaucratic wrangling with the local water board, Lawrence took a train for Cairo. He had to change trains at Ismaelia, where he caught sight of a party of senior officers walking up and down the platform. He recognised one of them as Burmester, an aide to Admiral Wemyss, who had flown his flag in the *Euryalus* off Wejh. Lawrence went and reported the capture of Aqaba. Burmester, a man of decision, at once arranged for the naval auxiliary *Dufferin* to take stores to Aqaba, and bring back the Turkish prisoners. That was not all, however. Lawrence also learned that the most imposing of the officers on the platform at Ismaelia was General Sir Edmund Allenby, who had come out to replace Murray as commander-in-chief.

Allenby was to emerge as probably the most successful commander of the First World War, but at this time his reputation was uncertain. Like so many others, he had bruised his skill on the unyielding problems of the Western Front: he was nicknamed The Bull, and not altogether because of his massive physical presence. There was a mutual antipathy between him and the British commander-in-chief, Sir Douglas Haig, dating back to rivalries of earlier soldering days. Allenby himself was unsure, and

**Turkish troops man a shallow defensive trench**

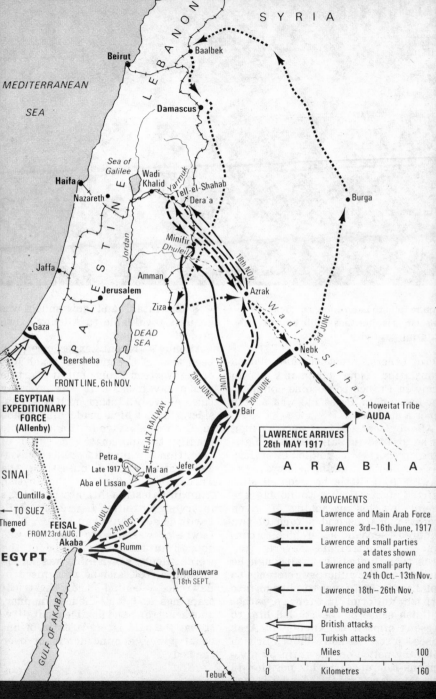

SYRIA

MEDITERRANEAN
SEA

Beirut
Baalbek
LEBANON

Damascus

Sea of
Galilee
Haifa
Wadi
Khalid
Nazareth
Yarmuk
Tell-el-Shahab
Dera'a
Burga

Minifir
Dhuleil
18th NOV.

Amman
Azrak

Jaffa
Jordan
Ziza

Jerusalem
Wadi

DEAD
SEA
3rd JUNE
Nebk
Sirhan

Gaza
Beersheba

FRONT LINE, 6th NOV.
22nd JUNE
20th JUNE
28th JUNE

EGYPTIAN
EXPEDITIONARY
FORCE
(Allenby)
Bair
Howeitat Tribe
AUDA

LAWRENCE ARRIVES
28th MAY 1917

HEJAZ RAILWAY

Petra
Late 1917
Ma'an
Jefer
A R A B I A

SINAI
Aba el Lissan

Quntilla
TO SUEZ
Themed
FEISAL
FROM 23rd AUG.
Akaba
Rumm

EGYPT
6th JULY
24th OCT
Mudauwara
18th SEPT.

MOVEMENTS

Lawrence and Main Arab Force
Lawrence 3rd–16th June, 1917
Lawrence and small parties
at dates shown
Lawrence and small party
24th Oct.–13th Nov.
Lawrence 18th–26th Nov.

Arab headquarters
British attacks
Turkish attacks

GULF OF AKABA

0        Miles        100
0     Kilometres     160

Tebuk

**Success at Aqaba – failure at the Yarmuk Bridge**

Aqaba falls to Lawrence's attack;
Turkish prisoners assemble before
entering captivity

were others, whether his sudden translation from command of an army in France to become commander-in-chief in Palestine was a step up or a step down.

Allenby sent for Lawrence as soon as he arrived in Cairo. It was, Lawrence reports, a comic interview, with Allenby looking sideways at Lawrence, 'a little bare-footed silk-skirted man offering to hobble the enemy by his preaching if given stores and arms and a fund of two hundred thousand sovereigns to convince and control his converts . . .' It is to be noted that, although he makes some perfunctory reference to not having had time to change into British uniform, Lawrence's rather childish sense of theatre led him to present himself to Allenby in Arab robes – just as he had annoyed British military police on the train by mysterious references to his position in the 'Meccan Army'. Allenby's task now, as Lawrence admits, was to decide just how much of Lawrence

was charlatan, and how much was genuinely valuable to Allenby's own projected campaign.

Allenby's recent experience had been that of the gun-and-trench war of the Western Front, but at heart he was a cavalryman. It was probably this, above all other military considerations, which made him decide in Lawrence's favour. He was able readily to appreciate the kind of operations which Lawrence envisaged, stinging and unsettling the Turks on the flank of the British front in Palestine. Allenby closed the interview by telling Lawrence: 'Well, I will do for you what I can.' This, Lawrence was now to discover, was enough in the fullest sense of the word. Allenby's own mind was powerful and direct, and he recognised in Lawrence, behind the theatrical trappings and false-modest manner, another strong and flexible mentality. It was, he said later, 'a brain of unusual power, a mind dominant over the body . . .'

**General Sir Edmund Allenby replaces Murray as C-in-C**

74

# The troop train

On the Palestine front, Allenby had inherited an indeterminate position from his predecessor. Murray, attacking at the end of 1916, had gradually, in a series of relatively minor engagements, cleared the whole of the Sinai Peninsula of Turkish forces. Thus he had made the whole position of Egypt immensely safer from Turkish attack. It might have been thought that this was sufficient achievement on a front far from that on which the ultimate decision of the war seemed likely to be reached. However, other considerations were brought into play during 1917. The fall of Jerusalem, it was believed, would be a heartening victory for the Allies in a year when victories were few – and it might also have a decisive effect upon opinion in the Arab world. After some urging from London, Murray carried his offensive into Palestine. Twice he attacked Gaza: twice, in confusion made worse by poor staff work, he failed. This was the situation which Allenby was brought from the Western Front to redeem.

From the first, Allenby resolv[e] not to continue mounting front[al] attacks on Gaza, but to use his gre[at] preponderance in cavalry – much of [the] Anzac forces – to outflank the tov[n] from inland. The main Turkish po[si]tion, with its right flank on the sea [at] Gaza, ran inland for about twen[ty] miles to the important wells [at] Beersheba. Allenby now planned [to] seize Beersheba by a sudden mob[ile] stroke, and then to envelop Gaza fro[m] the rear. He considerably outnu[m]bered the Turks: the German co[m]mander of the Turkish forces, v[on] Falkenhayn, was estimated to ha[ve] about 36,000 men generally availab[le] as against Allenby's 88,000. In caval[ry] Allenby could muster 16,500 sabr[es] against 2,000 Turkish, and in gu[ns] 433 against 258. Nevertheless, Allen[by] was contemplating an offensive [in] difficult country, against troops whi[ch] had twice flung back British forc[es] from the gates of Gaza. There w[as] also the prospect that more Turki[sh] troops of the best quality might so[on] be in Palestine, freed for service the[re] by the collapse of Rumania. T[he]

Turkish troops load supplies brought by train. The disruption of rail communications continues

heart of these potential reinforcements was a force which included 6,000 Germans. It was known by the codename of *Yilderim*, or Lightning, and had been originally intended to capture Baghdad. Thus it was of the greatest importance to Allenby that Turkish attention should be distracted from his impending *coup de main* at Beersheba and Gaza. Lawrence's projected operations on the Turkish flank, wrecking railways, sucking in garrison reinforcements, creating pro-Allied opinion amongst desert Arabs, were exactly what suited Allenby's own ideas. For bo Allenby and Lawrence, each was t right man at the right time.

For this new cooperation to wor it was necessary to bring Feisal, Arab commander-in-chief, more s curely within Allenby's orbi Lawrence now proposed that We; should be abandoned as a base, to l replaced by Aqaba, which – as l pointed out – was only about 130 mil from the British position at Wa Ghazze, whereas it was nearly 8 miles from Mecca. Feisal could al; be linked in with the British forc

on the Palestine front in a more personal sense – by making him an army commander under Allenby. This last move proved surprisingly easy to arrange. Lawrence journeyed to Jeddah to see Husein, whom he regarded as 'an obstinate, narrow-minded, suspicious character, little likely to sacrifice a pet vanity for unity of control.' However, Husein was most co-operative, seeing, as he thought, great advantages for his cause in the British alliance.

It is difficult to decide how far, in the late autumn of 1917, Lawrence still agreed with Husein over these advantages. In the after-the-event rationalisation to which Lawrence was often prone, he said after the war that '. . . not being a perfect fool, I could see that, if we won the war, the promises to the Arabs were dead paper. Had I been an honourable adviser I would have sent my men home, and not let them risk their

**Australian troops advance during the second battle of Gaza. Allenby forsook frontal attacks on the town in favour of outflanking tactics**

The German commander of the Turkish
forces, General von Falkenhayn,
conversing with a Turkish officer

ves for such stuff. Yet the Arab spiration was our main tool in inning the Eastern war. So I assured 1em that England kept her word in tter and spirit . . . I was continually tter and ashamed . . .'

This does not seem convincing. In ite of the post-war reference to 1y men' – ie, the Arabs – there is ttle indication that Lawrence at 1is time thought other than as a ritish officer, with much less of the lf-identification with the Arabs 1an legend afterwards proclaimed. awrence was also, on his own show-1g, a good enough military theorist know that the main tool in winning 1e Eastern war would not be 'the rab inspiration', useful though that ight be as an auxiliary aid. The ain tool would be General Sir dmund Allenby's 16,500 sabres. No 1erilla sideshow, however well run, uld match them in tactical or rategic importance.

It seems probable that Lawrence's riving force, at this period of his fe at least, was not so much pro-rab sentiment as anti-French. The *wenty-Seven Articles,* quoted earlier, veal no sense of identification with rabs, but stand rather as a quasi-1achiavellian manual on how to anipulate human beings of an alien 1ce. *Seven Pillars* contains many ferences to Lawrence's weariness of 1 things Arab, and his torment at 1ing alone in the part he had to play. oth he and Hogarth were certainly pposed to the Sykes-Picot agree-1ent, and the control of the Syrian 1ast which that agreement gave to rance. Hogarth and other members the Arab Bureau saw an inde-1ndent Arab state as being under ritish guidance, and they deplored 1e extension and deepening of French 1fluence in Syria. The question of ar between Britain and France did 1t seem then to be the fanciful 1atter it has since become, and it 1s one which greatly worried awrence, for whom French control Syria became something to be

fought and intrigued against and opposed in every way. In the very middle of the war, in March 1915, before he had begun his active role in the desert, we find Lawrence writing to Hogarth concerning his fears about French control of Syrian ports:

'. . . In the hands of France, it will provide a sure base for naval attacks on Egypt, and remember – with her [France] in Syria and compulsory service there, she will be able at any time to fling 100,000 men against the [Suez] canal in twelve days from the declaration of war . . .' In all his struggles with Bremond, it was an Arab as against a French Syria which Lawrence sought. It was defensive imperialism for Britain, rather than emergent nationalism for Arabia, which agitated his mind when he had time to think about the wider issues of his role.

However, as he talked with Husein at Jeddah, he had little time for these wider issues. On 17th July, he received two telegrams from Cairo. They told him that the Howeitat, on whom the defence of Aqaba now depended, had opened negotiations to transfer their allegiance to the Turks, and that they were being led in this by none other than Auda himself. Lawrence sailed at once for Aqaba in the naval auxiliary *Hardinge.* At Auda's headquarters, he greeted the old warrior and the Sherif Nasir, receiving a somewhat lame story about an attempt to deceive the Turks into parting with some money. Lawrence handled the affair brilliantly, joining in the rather thin laughter of Auda and his companions, but impressing the Arabs by his apparently detailed knowledge of negotiations they had imagined were secret. He did not lose his temper, or ride a high British horse with Auda. Instead, he gave him a present of gold, and promised him that Allenby was sending rifles, food, and more money. Auda decided that he preferred the reality of British golden

Turkish troops under inspection by a German officer. Allenby was concerned that strong reinforcements might arrive for the Turks, threatening the success of his attack on Beersheba and Gaza

1038

sovereigns to the uncertainties of Turkish pay.

Although Colonel Joyce was placed in nominal command at Aqaba, there is no doubt that from now onward the tactical and strategic driving force of Feisal's armies came from Lawrence. Lawrence's exploits were increasingly known among the desert tribes, told with exaggerations round many a thornwood fire. Aqaba had shown t Arabs that, properly advised, th could humiliate the Turks. Oth British soldiers in contact with t Bedouin at this time remember later the stir and bustle and impor ance of Lawrence's arrival in cam the cries of 'Aurens, Aurens,' (t Arab pronunciation of Lawrence name) and the excitement he cou

enerate in these volatile fighting
en.

Lawrence's strategic thinking at
his point was reasonably clear-cut.
e saw the war in the Hejaz as
nished, and the siege of Medina by
bdullah as little more than an
relevance. His hopes rested with
eisal, and he intended to use Feisal
'preach' the war north into Syria,
into settled lands where allegiance to
an Arab cause might be more firmly
based and less impulsive than among
the desert raiders. This had always
lain at the back of his thoughts. In
another letter of 1915 to Hogarth he
had stressed the chance that 'we can
rush right up to Damascus and biff
the French out of all hope of Syria.
It's a big game, and . . . worth trying

The troopship *Hardinge* in which Lawrence travelled to Aqaba to persuade Auda not to go over to the Turks

. . . ' In passing, it may be noted that this anti-French letter was written considerably more than a year before he himself began his personal mission in Arabia: the 'we' of the letter can only have meant Arabs under some kind of British tutelage. It was this prospect, distant and dreamlike in 1915, that had now, in the autumn of 1917, become a strategic reality.

However, war is tactics as well as strategy, and in the desert the two fuse into an almost indistinguishable whole. Lawrence's experiences so far had convinced him that the desert resembled the sea, and should be used like the sea – as a place from which to strike at will, a place into which to retire at will, a place in which to hide at will. He took for his guiding thought a remark by the 17th Century essayist, Francis Bacon: 'He who commands the sea is at great liberty, and may take as much or as little of the war as he will . . .' In such a war, the Bedouin had very considerable advantages. They knew the desert, its tracks, its contours, its wells, its moods of climate and of night and day. They could exist adequately

where men only a little more 'civil ised' might starve. Lawrence's raiding parties were designed to sting but not to annihilate; to loot and destroy but not to seize and occupy; to fight concentration of the conventional military kind by elusive dispersal of the traditional Arab kind.

The scale of rations and equipment which Lawrence gives for these raiding parties is almost unbelievably austere, and reveals sharply the privations which he, a Western man, must have endured while fighting his Arabian campaign. The raiders' vehicle was, of course, the camel, capable of 250 miles after watering and of a day's march varying between fifty and 110 miles. Each man carried forty-five pounds of flour slung on his riding saddle. This represented six weeks' rations – a capacity, says Lawrence, for a raid of 'a thousand miles out and back.' The water scale was even more derisory — a pint a man for emergency, or, for the less hardy among the raiders, for drinking between wells. The arms carried were simple: the essential, ubiquitous rifle, and the more sophisticated Hotchkiss and Lewis light automatic guns, plus, of course, the explosives and detonators used for demolition of the Turkish railway system. 'Ours,' said

Lawrence, 'were battles of minutes, fought at eighteen miles an hour.'

These raiding parties provided the basis for tactics which were brilliant enough of their kind – and perhaps the only tactics possible with the means at the disposal of Lawrence and Feisal. Yet they would not, in the last resort, be enough to 'biff' the Turks – or for that matter the French – out of Syria. It would need war of a more conventional kind for that.

The prospect of conventional war

Colonel Joyce with Feisal. The colonel's command of the forces at Aqaba was nominal; Lawrence was the moving spirit behind the Arabs' operations

began to loom above the Arabs soon after Lawrence's gift of £1,000 settled Auda's brief flirtation with the Turks. While Feisal and Joyce landed at Aqaba, Falkenhayn and the Turkish command began to strengthen their base at Ma'an in an effort to retake the port. As August ended, the Turkish force in Ma'an had become considerable – 6,000 infantry, a cavalry regiment, sixteen guns, and a squadron of aircraft operating from the nearby airfield. In addition, the wells at Abu Lissan, where Auda and Lawrence and Nasir had slaughtered

the Turkish battalion, had been re-occupied, with good defensive dug-in positions. They were now held by 2,000 men. Only Turkish nervousness after their recent reverse appeared to stand between them and the somewhat precariously held port of Aqaba.

Lawrence at once called in the most modern means to counter the Turkish threat. He asked Major-General Geoffrey Salmond, the British air commander in the Middle East, for a quick raid to disrupt Turkish preparations in Ma'an. The response was immediate. A flight was sent under Captain Stent, using an advanced landing ground at Quntilla, in east Sinai, about forty miles from Aqaba. The raid was carried out by the lumbering biplane bombers of the period, and was spectacularly successful. Coming in low over the Turkish perimeter at Ma'an. Stent's flight dropped thirty-two bombs. Eight hit the engine sheds; two struck the barracks, killing thirty-five men; four cratered and damaged the Turkish airfield; one fell on the Turkish commander's kitchen and killed his cook. All the British planes returned safely to Quntilla. Next day they went out again, and bombed the Tur-

Major-General Geoffrey Salmond, British air commander in the Middle East, cooperated with Lawrence and disrupted the build up of Turkish preparations with successful air attacks

A railway raiding party;
standing, left: Lieutenant-Colonel
Newcombe, right: Lieutenant
Hornby

kish horse line at Abu Lissan – returning a third time in the afternoon to destroy an anti-aircraft battery which had caused them some damage – but no casualties – in the earlier raid. It had been a distinctly upsetting forty-eight hours for the Turks.

The Turkish forces also had an unpleasant setback when they attempted to move into Petra, well to the north of Aqaba, where the Bedouin leader Maulud, an old, tried desert fighter, had established good guerilla positions with a mule-mounted force of a couple of hundred Arab soldiers, assisted by local tribesmen. Petra was an easy position to defend, and the Turkish choice of it as an area for counterattack was strange: presumably it was felt by the Turkish command that it would, if captured, in some way unhinge the Arab position farther south. Whatever the reasoning, the outcome was a Turkish disaster, though on a small scale. Sniping from the famous rose-red ruins, Maulud's men destroyed a Turkish company. A little more had been done to blunt the edge of enemy enthusiasm to try conclusions at Aqaba.

As an additional distraction, however, Lawrence had now decided on a major railway raid. The objective he chose was the station at Mudauwara, a water point for trains, about eighty miles from Aqaba. He took with him two British gun instructors to handle the machine gun and Stokes mortars he intended to use. These were both NCOs – the machine-gunner, Yells, was an Englishman and the mortar expert, Brooke, was an Australian. Lawrence nicknamed them Lewis and Stokes, after their respective weapons, and watched amusedly to see how they managed the Bedouin. He discovered that the Australian at

Auda ibn Zaal in his tent. Distrust of
Auda by one Howeitat clan threatens
the outcome of the Mudauwara station
raid

once dealt with the tribesmen in-
formally and directly, but was surprisingly annoyed when they
responded in the same way to him,
whereas the Englishman, insular and
shy, became more and more formally
correct in his dealing with the Arabs,
eliciting from them a wary respect.

The little expedition soon ran into
difficulty. The Howeitat, under Lawrence's plan, were to supply an escort
of 300 men. However, the particular
clan from whom these were to be
recruited on the way to Mudauwara
turned out to be bitterly jealous and
distrustful of Auda, and unwilling to
help any enterprise with which he
was associated. In desperation,
Lawrence rode back to Feisal's headquarters in Aqaba, and managed to
get a mediator to return with him to
his halting place at Rumm. After a
long wrangle, the rebellious Howietat
decided to supply a hundred men,
instead of the 300 for whom they had
been asked. On 16th September, the
expedition set out once more for
Mudauwara, though the atmosphere
was poisoned by lack of trust and by
tribal jealousies.

When evening came, Lawrence went
out on reconnaissance with Zaal and
the two British sergeants, and closed
in to within a few yards of the Turkish
tents at the station. They watched
an officer come out and light a cigar-
ette, and heard his men talking
inside their tents. The garrison
seemed to consist of about 200 men –
roughly double the size of Lawrence's
force – and the station buildings
were solid stone which were proof
against a Stokes shell. Lawrence
decided that an attack on the station
might well be a costly failure under
these circumstances. The following
day the Arabs marched down the line,
disturbing herds of oryx and gazelle,
looking for a suitable site on which

88

they could destroy a Turkish train. The mortar sergeant, 'Stokes', rode with difficulty, since he had contracted dysentery from drinking suspect water. At last they found their killing ground, where the line curved above a culvert.

The Stokes mortar and the machine guns were positioned on a high ledge above the line, while Lawrence put fifty pounds of gelatine explosive into the line above the culvert. The work took five hours, but at last it was done, with 200 yards of cable leading to a firing position on a ridge. It was now dusk, and the Bedouin settled down to wait – never the easiest task for them, and certainly the military virtue which they most lacked. Squatting foolishly on the skyline at sunset, despite Lawrence's angry orders, they finally attracted the attention of a Turkish post to the south, which broke into a flurry of anxious shots.

However, there were no further alarms until morning came. Then, at about nine o'clock, a Turkish patrol, about forty strong, began to advance down the line. Lawrence was in a quandary. The Bedouin, with their superior numbers, could probably drive away the patrol, but if they did so, the Turkish commander would certainly warn the railway operating staff not to send a train into the suspect area. On the other hand, if the Bedouin fell back in front of the Turks, they would be unable to detonate the mine under any train that might appear. The problem was finally solved by detaching about a quarter of Lawrence's force, and sending them to skirmish on the Turkish flanks, gradually luring the Turks away from the line into the broken hilly country beyond it.

This was not the end of Turkish activity. A small line patrol of a corporal and eight men came along the railway beneath the Bedouin positions, but passed without noticing anything out of the ordinary. Worse was to follow. At noon Lawrence,

watching Mudauwara station throug his field glasses, saw a hundred me form up and begin a slow approac towards the Arab position. Lawrenc was just about to give up in despai when a look-out cried that he coul see smoke in the distance. The lon awaited train was coming. The Aral scrambled back into position.

The train must have been an extra ordinary sight – two powerful engine with ten box-wagons, the windows which bristled with rifle muzzl firing sporadically into the empt desert. On the roofs of the box wagor little sandbagged positions had bee built, where Turkish riflemen peere anxiously out across the sand ar scrub. Lawrence crouched on a hilloc near the culvert, waiting to give t signal to an Arab who waited besi the exploder 200 yards away. As t second engine rumbled on to t little bridge, Lawrence raised h hand.

The explosion was devastatin Almost the whole of the secor engine was blown to pieces – lumps iron and steel, including a who locomotive wheel, curving high ov the Arabs' heads to crash far behir them into the desert. The wago were strewn along the track, a already the Bedouin were pouri rifle fire into the Turks trying scramble to the cover of the emban ment. With a stuttering roar, t Lewis guns opened up, scything t Turks from the tops of the derail wagons. Some of the Turkish infant ran desperately into the hollow und the culvert. The second shot from t Stokes gun landed in the middle them, killing twenty and woundi many more. The battle was over. had taken ten minutes.

Beside the wreck, the Bedou seemed to have gone mad in th lust for loot. Stores and goods l everywhere – carpets, clothes, cooki pots, weapons, money. Small grou of survivors huddled together. crowd of about forty screami women implored Lawrence for p

tion, though the Arabs were too
sy loading the camels with more
terial advantages to bother about
em. Lawrence promised them that
e Turks from Mudauwara would
on be with them – a forecast which
knew might well be only too
curate. Less fortunate was a party
Austrian officers and NCOs who
ked for quarter. Lawrence granted
s, but within a few minutes most
re dead, cut down while his back
s turned because of some unex-
ined dispute with a group of
douin.

houting and quarrelling, the
douin loaded the camels and made
into the desert. All military co-
sion was now lost: the dissensions
ich had lain beneath the surface
the raiding force meant that it
not have the comradely unity of
er more homogenous parties. The
nels on which Lawrence and the
o sergeants were to escape did not
pear – long ago seized by the tribes-
n to carry extra plunder. Gradually
ence fell round the wrecked train,
ere Lawrence stood with the two
tish sergeants, alone. Luckily,
al had retained a sense of responsi-
ity. He rode back with two camels,
ile the English sergeant went out
found a stray. The Australian,
ak with dysentery, was pushed
oss one of the camels, while the
er beasts took the Stokes gun and
Lewis guns. It was a race against
e, for the Turkish force from
dauwara was now spreading out on
flanks, moving cautiously but
nly on the scene of the wreck, un-
tain of the strength of the Bedouin
ce. Zaal and the English sergeant
fire to a heap of Turkish ammuni-
n, and the resulting crackle of
losions disconcerted the Turks,
o apparently thought that the
ots came from some well-organised
ence. They paused to make a
rough reconnaissance, and Law-
ce and Zaal and the others slipped
ay.

ven so, all was not over yet. When
he rejoined the main party, Lawrence
found that the man who had actually
fired the mine, Salem, was missing.
He rode back with Zaal and a dozen
men, but found that there were so
many Turks round the wrecked train
by this time that to search for Salem
was quite impossible. In fact,
Lawrence's rescue party was almost
cut off, but was saved by the admirable
sergeant whom Lawrence had chris-
tened Lewis. He suddenly appeared in
support, mounted on a camel, with a
machine gun held across his thighs.
The Turks withdrew. Later Lawrence
found that Salem, who was wounded,
had been picked up by another Arab.
'He bore me,' Lawrence recorded
later, 'always a little grudge for
having left him behind, when he was
of my company and wounded. I had
failed in staunchness . . .'

The afternoon's work had cost the
Turks seventy dead, thirty wounded,
and eighty prisoners – in addition to
two valuable locomotives. One Arab
had been killed and a handful
wounded – none seriously. In a letter
written to a British officer at the
time, Lawrence sounds excited and
cheerful at this taste of action:

'I hope this sounds the fun it is. The
only pity is the sweat to work them
up and the wild scramble while it
lasts. It's the most amateurish,
Buffalo-Billy sort of performance, and
the only people who do it well are the
Bedouin. Only you will think it is
heaven, because there aren't any
returns, or orders, or superiors, or
inferiors; no doctors, no accounts, no
meals, and no drinks . . .'

Two others who had done well,
however, were the English machine
gunner and the Australian mortar
man. On their return to Aqaba, they
were recalled to Cairo. Lawrence paid
them a slightly patronising tribute:

'They had won a battle single-
handed; had had dysentery; lived on
camel-milk; and learned to ride a
camel fifty miles a day without pain.
Also Allenby gave them a medal
each . . .'

Lawrence teaches Arabs how to use the Stokes mortar

# The nightmare

The work on the railway mounted in scope and in intensity. The Aqaba raiding group destroyed seventeen Turkish trains during the next four months: the engine drivers went on strike: those passengers who had to travel south on the Hejaz line paid extra money for seats in the rearmost wagons. The most effective of these raids, however, came near to ending Lawrence's life. On 6th September, accompanied by a French captain, Pisani, he blew up a train near Ma'an, killing twenty Turks, but was nicked in the hip by a bullet from a Turkish colonel blazing away with a Mauser from a carriage window. It was daring, dazzling, but it was not enough to win campaigns. Suddenly, Allenby reminded Lawrence of this.

Lawrence was summoned to Cairo. If he had imagined he was going to get the wary respect he had received from Allenby on his first meeting, he was wrong. Allenby was now preparing for his Beersheba-Gaza thrust, and

hoping to go on to seize Jerusalem: couple of companies of Turks kill far away on the Hejaz line did n impress him as a worthwhile effort aid his own strategic and tactic plans. In *Seven Pillars*, Lawrence always careful to give Allenby fu praise as 'the man the men work for, the image we worshipped . . Nevertheless, he must have found h meeting with the commander-in-chi somewhat disconcerting. Allen asked him directly what he felt l was achieving with his pin-pri raids, or, in Lawrence's own wor 'if they meant anything at all beyor the melodramatic advertisement th gave Feisal's cause.' Lawrence, forc to defend himself in the kind of situ tion where he always liked to attac replied by putting forward his theo that by constantly harassing t Hejaz railway line, but not closing entirely, he would keep the Turki

**Lawrence at Aqaba**

**A German-built Turkish locomotive captured by Australian troops. Lawrence's activities with his Arabs resulted in the destruction of seventeen trains in four months**

command supplying a useless garrison in Medina, where it would cost the Allies much less money than if it were in prison camps in Egypt.

This clever but esoteric reasoning was not enough for Allenby. He was thinking in wider terms. He wanted something more directly helpful to his plans – and something which was heavier in weight. What he proposed was an Arab uprising in the north, around Damascus. This would be supported by an offensive by Feisal's Arab troops, and timed to coincide with his own Gaza-Beersheba offensive. Lawrence tells us that he turned this down. How far it was possible for him to do this – it must be remembered that he was a lowly major and Allenby a scarlet general – is at this distance in time very difficult to decide. In *Seven Pillars* Lawrence writes of the decision rather as though it were one reluctantly given by one commander-in-chief to another. In fact, it is rather more likely that Allenby, who knew an intelligent expert when he saw one, accepted Lawrence's *advice* on the matter, and made the decision himself. The reasoning behind Lawrence's advice could not all have been given to Allenby – part of it was, as Lawrence wrote later, that 'Allenby was quite untried'. Nevertheless, the rest of his argument was cogent enough – basically that although the Arabs might possibly take the vital rail junction of Deraa in the north, and even Damascus itself, they might not be able to hold them if Allenby was rebuffed round Gaza. A successful Turkish counterattack in these settled areas, where there was no desert into which rebel Arabs could easily escape, would end in the slaughter of all those Arabs who rose in Feisal's cause, and bring the

whole Arab Revolt into discredit and eventual ruin. This would not only have destroyed Feisal's political position – something which Allenby, preoccupied with the realities of a great campaign, might not have worried about unduly – but it would also have been, at the very least, a great nuisance to the British war effort. This latter argument was probably decisive with Allenby.

However, something still had to be done. It was in these circumstances, under some pressure to prove his usefulness to his commander-in-chief, that Lawrence decided on his boldest stroke yet – a plan, rather less carefully worked out than those of his lesser operations along the railway, to blow a vital bridge over the River Yarmuk, which lay between Deraa and the Sea of Galilee. With the bridge out of commission, the Turkish forces in Palestine would be cut off from their bases round Damascus, and there would be no troop trains either for escape or for reinforcement. From Allenby's point of view, this was certainly better than nothing: he agreed, and asked that the bridge should be blown on 5th November, or any one of the three days following. This would suit him well, since he intended to open his Gaza-Beersheba attack on the last day of October.

The Yarmuk raid was a most daring conception, and one which drives home sharply Lawrence's view of his own campaign as a quasi-naval war. The distance scale was prodigious – no less than a 420-mile march from Aqaba, through enemy country, relying on the unquantifiable assistance of tribes on the route. Even the explosive technique was quite new to Lawrence, since the destruction of the great steel girders of Yarmuk was a very different matter from blowing up railway culverts. In view of this,

Lawrence took with him on the raid a Royal Engineer officer, Wood, who was base engineer at Aqaba. Wood was eager to go, in spite of the fact that he was not considered fit for active operations, having been shot through the head on the Western Front earlier in the war. It was proposed to use 'necklaces' of gelatine explosive, detonated electrically .

Among the most important of the Arabs in the party were two men, one whom Lawrence immensely liked and respected, and one whom he distrusted. The former was Ali ibn el Husein, a young sheik who was released by Feisal for the task since Nasir was away from Aqaba. The sheer exuberant manhood of the young Ali seemed to catch Lawrence's imagination. He wrote of him enthusiastically as a man who could carry a man on the palm of each hand, and who could outdistance a trotting camel over half a desert mile, and then leap into the saddle. More to the point than these unusual accomplishments, he had also acquired considerable experience at railway demolition under Newcombe farther south.

Less welcome was Abd el Kader, an Algerian *emir*. He was the grandson of the man who had fought the French in Algeria earlier in the preceding century – a fact which by itself might have been expected to get at least a benevolent nod from Lawrence. Moreover, he could be important, since he controlled the allegiance of groups of exiled Algerian Arabs who lived along the banks of the Yarmuk. But he was a jerky, febrile character, burning with religious bigotry, and his stories of his past activities did not tally with such facts as were known about him. Moreover, even as the raiding party waited to set out, a telegram arrived from Lawrence's old opponent, Colonel Bremond. Abd el Kader, warned Bremond, was in the pay of the Turks. Lawrence trusted Bremond even less than he trusted Abd el Kader, however, and the *emir* was

99

allowed to go with the raiders. It was, as will be seen, a mistake. As they set out from Aqaba on 24th October, Feisal, too, had whispered a qualified warning to Lawrence about Abd el Kader: 'I know he is mad. I think he is honest. Guard your heads and use him'.

The first stage of the journey was through Rumm to old Auda's camp at Jefer. Lawrence was accompanied by a section of Indian machine gunners, whose duty it would be to hold the approaches to the Yarmuk bridge while the explosives were fixed in position and detonated. From the first, it was an ill-starred venture. Wood fell ill early in the journey, for which he was now demonstrably physically unfit. Ali and Abd el Kader quarrelled jealously, bitterly, and incessantly. When, finally, the raiders rode into Auda's tents in the bushy brushwood near the wells on the Jefer plain, Auda was not at his best. He, too, was quarrelling with surrounding clans – as usual, about money. Lawrence also found that the arch-raider, Zaal, whom he had hoped to enlist for the trip with some of the Abu Tayi, was unwilling to go. According to Lawrence, he had changed from 'the hard-riding gallant of spring into a prudent man, whose new wealth made life precious to him . . .' But it was old Auda himself who sowed the last seed of unease. As he clasped Lawrence to him in farewell, he muttered through his beard: 'Beward of Abd el Kader'.

Slowly the little party pushed on. The Indians were not born to the saddle like the Bedouin, and they did not have the will-power of Lawrence and Wood. They could make only about thirty-five miles a day. Lawrence must have found the time factor looming larger and larger above him, for on the previous evening, talking in Auda's tent, he had felt the ground tremble, and had heard

**Turkish troops in forward positions before Allenby's attack on Beersheba**

the rumble of Allenby's guns as
they opened their preliminary, decep-
tive barrage upon Gaza. After a
brief but bloodless clash with the
Beni Sakhr tribe, Ali and Lawrence
recruited the local chief, Mifleh and
fifteen of his tribesmen for the expedition — though the objective was
said vaguely to a 'a raid' and not
specifically the Yarmuk bridge. On
4th November, after picking up more
followers from the Serahin tribe,
they reached the ancient oasis of
Azrak, once a fort of Rome. At the
same time, Abd el Kader disappeared,
with all his seven followers. It looked
very much as though he might be
about to inform the Turks of the impending attack on the Yarmuk bridge.

The bridge which Lawrence had now
decided to attack was that at Tell
el-Shahab, since the other possible
bridge at Wadi Khalid was not possible

**Captain Wood of the Royal Engineers,
Lawrence's explosive expert on the
Yarmuk expedition**

**The Yarmuk rail bridge in Syria, target for Lawrence's unsuccessful sabotage attempt of June 1917**

without the local help of Abd el Kader. Tell el-Shahab meant a formidable round trip of eighty miles. Lawrence chose the six hardiest Indians, with one machine gun. The Arab force for the final assault consisted of twenty Beni Sakhr and forty Serahin, with Lawrence's small bodyguard in addition. They set off at night on 6th November, watching the glow of the station lights at Deraa to the north of them, riding silently through a dismal drizzle of rain, the camels floundering in the mud. At last they heard, louder and louder, the roar of the river in the

Yarmuk gorge. They had reached t[ objective.

The bridge was only lightly hel for the Turks had not seriously a ticipated a raid so far behind their lin In a later report to the *Arab Bullet* in Cairo, Lawrence estimated th the guardpost could be rushed ' twenty decent men'. However, it w not to be. Lawrence crawled forwa until he could almost touch t bridge, where a single sentry w pacing up and down. At that momer one of the Arabs behind Lawren dropped his rifle, which clatter down the rocks. The sentry swu round, fired a hurried round, a turned out the guard. Above La rence, fatally, the Beni Sak answered with a ragged volley.

As they made their way back to Asrak, Ali - anxious to try to save something from the wreck of their hopes - suggested that they should try to blow a train. Lawrence was not especially enthusiastic, since it would have to be a hurried and inadequately planned attempt. However, the Serahin had still got a bag or two of gelignite, and Lawrence had the electric detonators. Eventually, he agreed, and on 10th November they laid a mine at Minifir, near which Lawrence had worked earlier in the year. A troop train approached but rumbled harmlessly over the mine. The detonator had failed. Fortunately, although Lawrence had been seen from the train, a patrol which returned from it to search the track where he had been sitting failed to find the wires. Furiously disappointed, Lawrence and the Arabs waited until next day - and were rewarded by a richer prize. Lawrence blew up a two-engined troop train, pulling twelve passenger coaches. One of them was beflagged, and looked important. It was later learned that this contained Mehmed Jemal Pasha, commanding the Turkish Eighth Army Corps, on his way to reinforce Jerusalem against Allenby. Watched by their corps commander, the troops from the train fought spiritedly, and the Arabs withdrew without much loot. They killed some dozens of Turks, but lost seven dead. All these were killed when the resourceful Ali, seeing Lawrence fall after being hit by a piece of the train on his right foot, charged down the hill to the rescue under heavy fire. Ali was a friend worth having.

The Yarmuk disappointment proved a traumatic incident for Lawrence. He was beginning to suffer, not only from the strain and hardship of his physical role in the campaign, but also from the confusion of his thoughts. He worried about 'betrayal' of the Arabs: he worried about what he was going to say next time he met Allenby. A letter to a friend at this

orm of fire broke out between Turks d Bedouin blazing blindly into the rkness. Then came the *coup-de-âce* to the whole Yarmuk scheme. e Serahin, who were carrying the cks of gelatine, had learned in other ys what happened when explosive s hit by bullets. They promptly rled their sacks into the gorge and d. There was nothing left for wrence to do but to try to escape. ey all managed to do so, but it was bitterly disillusioned party which le back from the Yarmuk. 'Our nds,' said Lawrence, 'were sick th failure.' In the distance, as ough to mark Lawrence's lack of ccess, he could hear Allenby's guns pporting forward some attack by e British forces to the south.

ne reveals his near-despair:

I'm not going to last out this game
uch longer, nerves going and temper
earing thin ... On a show so narrow
d voracious as this, one loses one's
st and one's balance, and becomes
pelessly self-centred. I don't think
ever think except about shop, and
n quite certain I never do anything
se . . . This killing and killing of
irks is horrible. When you charge in
the finish, and find them all over
e place in bits, and still alive many
them, and know that you have done
ndreds in the same way before and
ist do hundreds more if you can . . .'
t was Lawrence's peculiar and
rrifying tragedy that this black
ood of his life was now to be over-
adowed by an act of personal dese-
ition such as few men are called
on to endure. Possibly as some sort
sop for the Yarmuk failure, pos-
ly to give himself action as a rest
m thought, he set out from Azrak
e in November to make a recon-
issance to the south.

.awrence had chosen as his objec-
e the important railway junction
Deraa, whose lights he had seen on
e disastrous Yarmuk venture. He
velled on foot, with only one
mpanion, and he wore old shabby
es instead of his customary
erifian white silk. He walked right
wn into Deraa, mentally listing
e piles of stores behind the barbed
re compounds, the Albatross
hters parked in the hangars of the
field, the positions of trenches and
n posts. Suddenly there was a shout.
wrence and his companion walked
pefully on, but a Turkish sergeant
i after them and caught Lawrence
the arm, saying: 'The Bey wants
i.' He was taken to a guard room
i questioned. To account for his
r skin and blue eyes, he said he was
ircassian from Kuneitra, believing
it such a man would not be subject

to military service. This plea, however, was ignored, and Lawrence was
forcibly enrolled as a private in the
Turkish army. After dark, the
Governor of Deraa, Nahi Bey, sent
for him. He was taken to the Bey's
bedroom, where he was told that his
first duty in the Turkish army would
be to submit to the Bey's sexual
desires. When Lawrence resisted, he
succeeded in causing such agony to
the Bey that the Turk gasped out to
the guard to have Lawrence flogged.
He was beaten until he was bloodily
unconscious, but, according to his
own account, he remembered to cry
out in Arabic. When he was dragged
back to the Bey's bed, he was rejected
as too ghastly an object for sexual
attention, and the corporal of the
guard was ordered to take his place.
Lawrence was taken back to a hut
where he was bandaged and left alone.
In the morning, soon after dawn, he
walked out of the hut, unimportant
and unnoticed, and escaped through
the town and out of the valley to the
south. When he rejoined his companions, he said nothing of what
happened, but rode 'gently and carefully' to Azrak. On the following day
he began a 300-mile camel ride back
to Aqaba, a journey which he completed in under seventy hours. That,
summarised, is Lawrence's own account of what happened to him in
Deraa. It is a story which some com-
mentators do not believe.

Richard Aldington, for instance,
quotes a letter written by Lawrence
to Mrs Bernard Shaw in March 1924
in which he admitted that he had
finally given way to the Bey.

'. . . For fear of being hurt,' said the
letter, 'or rather, to earn five minutes'
respite from a pain that drove me
mad, I gave away the only possession
we are born into the world with – our
bodily integrity . . . You may call this
morbid: but think of the offence, and
the intensity of my brooding over it
for these years. It will hang about me
while I live, and afterwards if our
personality survives . . .'

whether it happened in the way described by Lawrence. Inquiries made about the Bey (who died in 1965) establish that he was certainly a man who liked girls, and had a formidably heterosexual reputation. However, the Turkish sexual habits of the period would not have inhibited him from homosexual activity. More to the point, perhaps, are those doubters who say that after such a flogging Lawrence could not possibly have made the great ride back to Aqaba within forty-eight hours. Here, however, Lawrence is saved by his own reputation. His most outstanding characteristic, to those who knew him well, was the way in which his body was made to serve his will. He had already demonstrated, several times, an ability to out-do, out-last, out-ride any Bedouin – and the Bedouin are one of the most hardy races in the world. Moreover, Lawrence describes this ride in agonising terms.

'. . . I found myself,' he wrote, 'dividing into parts. There was one which went on riding wisely, sparing or helping every pace of the camel. Another hovering above and to the right bent down curiously, and asked what the flesh was doing. The flesh gave no answer, for, indeed, it was conscious only of a ruling impulse to keep on and on . . .'

All in all, in spite of the doubts, it is difficult not to come to the conclusion that what Lawrence described at Deraa *did* happen – and much as he described it. To invent such an episode, depicted in such terms, is an unlikely piece of mendacity. What is certainly true is that after Deraa, Lawrence's personality changed, becoming in some respects harder, less boyish, than his early wartime letters made him out to be. Those who saw him ride into Aqaba said that he looked like a ghost.

his hardly affects the credibility awrence's basic story. It would be ectly understandable if Lawrence se not to reveal the ultimate or of that night. To such a man – ny human being – rape would be a l degradation, and the business of ;ing down what happened on er would be clouded by all sorts deeply personal considerations. er commentators, however, have bted whether the Deraa incident pened at all – or, at any rate,

el Kader. Friction and distrust erated by this Algerian emir acterised the Yarmuk sabotage mpt; eventually he deserted with nen

Allenby's offensive in the south is
supported by machine-gunners.
Lawrence heard the noise of battle from
Yarmuk after retiring from the scene of
the Yarmuk bridge debacle.

# The armoured war

Recalled to see Allenby, Lawrence was lucky. He was flown to the commander-in-chief's headquarters which were now north of Gaza. By this time the Gaza victory was an assured fact, and Allenby was pressing the Turks back to Jerusalem. Headquarters was full of confident victory talk, and Lawrence's brief report of his failure at the Yarmuk was received without undue inquiry, and without any recrimination. Indeed, Lawrence was still at Allenby's headquarters when Jerusalem fell, and Allenby generously asked him to be present when he officially entered the city, on foot, on 11th December. Rigged out in the red tabs and khaki of a staff major, borrowed from friends at headquarters, he joined the ceremony of entry at the Jaffa Gate. 'For me,' he said later, 'it was the supreme moment of the war . . .'

However, supreme moment or not, the war was far from finished. Allenby's troops were having a diffi-cult time in the hills around Jeruslem. He now wanted Feisal's Ara army to move on the Dead Sea, a vancing on the town of Tafila, whic was a food base for the Dead Sea gra ships whose cargoes were distribute to Turkish forces by the Hejaz rai way. Lawrence readily fell in with th plan, which would, of course, brin both him and Feisal to the wid stage of which he was beginning i creasingly to dream.

A new technique of warfare was al beginning to grip him. He had alrea enthused over the speed and rang of his camel raids 'at eighteen mil an hour'; he had armed his came like light raiding craft with machi gun crews of two men, who sometim fired from the saddle. Indeed, he hi self had used an air Lewis gu stripped down to its bare essentia mounted in a bucket on his sadd firing widely dispersed 'groups' rounds at suitable targets. Now, last, these flesh-and-blood machi

'... all the Turks in Arabia could not fight one armoured car in open country.' Lawrence saw the opportunity of extending traditional Arab hit-and-run tactics with these vehicles

Turkish officials under guard after the fall of Jerusalem

gun carriers were being supplemented by the invention which had already begun to change the face of the 20th Century – the internal combustion engine. Among the stores now being unloaded at Aqaba, in preparation for the move to the north, were armoured cars . . . Fords, Rolls-Royces, Talbots, with British crews. They suited Lawrence in two ways. They were admirably constituted to fit in with his theories of desert war, and, from a personal point of view, they fed what was to become one of the ruling passions of his life – the love of speed.

At the end of December, Lawrence tried out the cars with a quick raid on isolated Turkish positions near Mudauwara, giving the Turks a fright, and convincing himself – if he needed convincing – of their military value. The driver of Lawrence's own Rolls-Royce – himself, incidentally, named

**Allenby's official entry into Jerusalem, at which Lawrence was present on the general's invitation**

Rolls – has given a vivid account of Lawrence's immense satisfaction in swift movements over the desert flats.

'. . . TE took his seat at my side . . . He pumped me as to the speed that could be obtained, given fair surface; I said I would show him at the first opportunity. This soon came; after traversing some forty miles we plunged between the tall rocks of Rum, crashed over soft sand dunes, then he shouted, "Here we are". For stretching away as far as I could see was the vast mud plain of Jefer, glinting white, looking like a beach disappearing to the sea, but this was only a mirage; forty miles of baked-hard, dead-level surface. TE had a craze for speed and with delight he watched our speedometer, 30-40-50-60-70 – there was nothing here to stop one travelling at any speed; other cars came along and TE shouted encouragement . . .'

Behind his excitement, however, Lawrence was thinking. He realised that with the cars, raiding parties could travel from Guweira to the railway line in a single day, leaving traffic completely at the raiders' mercy. He reasoned, correctly, that 'all the Turks in Arabia could not fight one armoured car in open country'. It was certainly an advanced doctrine, for its day, of armoured war – but it must be admitted that Lawrence was given an ideal stage on which to display its advantages.

Sir Basil Liddell Hart gives Lawrence enormous credit for his vision in this respect, saying that he was at least a generation ahead of the military world in perceiving the strategic implications of mechanised warfare – just as his machine gun camels had in a sense anticipated the tracked Bren-gun carriers of the 1930s and Second World War. Without denying Lawrence considerable credit for his sure intellectual grasp of the military theory needed to deal with local conditions in Arabia, one might legitimately doubt if his theories were, in fact, more widely based. Lawrence was fighting a war quite different in kind from that being fought anywhere else in the world. It was another world from the struggle of Haig and Foch in France and Flanders. It was even very different from the problem which confronted Allenby north of Gaza.

Nothing could better have illustrated the intensely personal nature of Lawrence's war than the so-called 'bodyguard' with which he was equipping himself. This force finally numbered ninety men, led by a famous Ageyl raider, Abdulla el Nahabi. Each was a picked rider, mounted on a crack camel. They wore a variety of bright colours, but never white, for that was Lawrence's colour. Each was paid £6 a month by Lawrence.

This was the normal wage for a tribesman who provided his own camel: since Lawrence provided the camels for his bodyguard, the money was excellent. By the end of the war, according to Lawrence, nearly sixty of them had died in his service. They formed, for Lawrence, not only a bodyguard but a small, trustworthy mobile reserve whom he could use in a crisis.

However, it was with a rather more conventional stroke of warfare that the Sherif Nasir first captured Tafila, as Allenby desired. Operating in intensely cold, snowy weather – in which ten of his men died of exposure – he seized the station at Jurf, thirty

**Stores for Arab and Allied troops arrive at Aqaba**

miles north of Ma'an. Then, taking a mounted force through the night and the snow, he received the surrender of Tafila's small garrison of 150 Turkish soldiers. At this point, the eternal, centrifugal tendencies of the Bedouin reasserted themselves. They were not an army, they were a collection of armed tribes, and they began to quarrel. At length, Auda – whose very name had induced the surrender of Tafila – rode back with his followers into the desert. He left Tafila to be held by Lawrence's bodyguard, about a hundred Arab regular troops from the forces of Feisal's brother Zeid, and some Algerian and Egyptian machine-gunners. The Turks at once attacked – three battalions of infantry, not fully up to strength; a hundred cavalry; two howitzers; and

ear view of a Rolls-Royce armoured
r. Armoured cars of a number of
arques, including RRs, arrived at
qaba in December 1917

*Blue Mist,* Lawrence's own Rolls-Royce, in the Wadi Ithm

a couple of dozen machine guns. On 24th January, this Turkish force had rolled up the outlying Arab skirmish line, and was threatening to retake Tafila.

The commander of the Tafila garrison was Zeid. He was eager to pull back his force to a ravine south of the town, where he believed they had a better defensive position. Lawrence disagreed. In the panic and confusion of the Turkish onslaught, under a heavy fire from the enemy howitzers, the command gradually slipped from Zeid to Lawrence. Lawrence had always avoided pitched battle, which did not come within the set of principles he had set for desert war. The battle he fought now was one which he later described, bitterly, as a 'parody'. According to him, he had raked up from the depths of his mind the half-forgotten classical precepts of war learned from his earlier reading, and had put them into action on the slopes of Tafila.

In effect, he adopted a Cannae-like plan, luring the Turks forward against a progressively retiring centre, and then attacking their exposed flanks with riflemen and cavalry. When the centre broke, it was chased from the field by armed villagers. The Turkish dead were estimated at about 1,000. They had lost both howitzers, and all the machine guns. The Arab losses were, according to Lawrence, 'twenty or thirty of our six hundred men, and the wounded would be perhaps three times as many . . .'

In later life, Lawrence usually affected to despise himself for having fought this battle, when, according to himself, he could have achieved the same result by out-manoeuvring the Turks, saving hundreds of Turkish and Arab lives. This does not show in the official report of the day, however, though Lawrence later covered himself against this charge by denigrating, in *Seven Pillars,* the very report

he had made for his superiors at head quarters. At the time, the battle c Tafila was a success: it was wha Allenby had asked for: and, incident ally, it won Lawrence the Distin guished Service Order to add to hi CB.

Moreover, within three day Lawrence himself demonstrated ho the victory in this pitched batt could be used to forward Arab an Allied plans, and how it could be use as a launching pad for an operatio of a more traditionally Lawrence-lik type. He proposed to follow up th

rkish local disaster at Tafila by
iding the Dead Sea port of Kerak,
 destroy a flotilla of Turkish
hters which was bound for the
rthern Turkish base at Jericho.
venty tribesmen, horse-mounted,
ooped down on Kerak in the cold
wn of 28th January, flustering the
rks into surrender, burning the
ts, plundering the supplies,

e fast, mobile Bren gun carrier of
er years was anticipated in
wrence's use of camel-mounted
chine-guns

**British Rolls-Royce 1914 Admiralty Turreted Pattern armoured car**
*Weight:* 3.5 tons. *Crew:* 3. *Armament:* one .303-inch Vickers Maxim machine-gun
*Armour:* 8mm. *Engine:* Rolls-Royce 50hp. *Speed:* 50mph. *Range:* 150 miles.
*Length:* 16 feet 9 inches. *Width:* 6 feet 3 inches. *Height:* 7 feet 7 inches

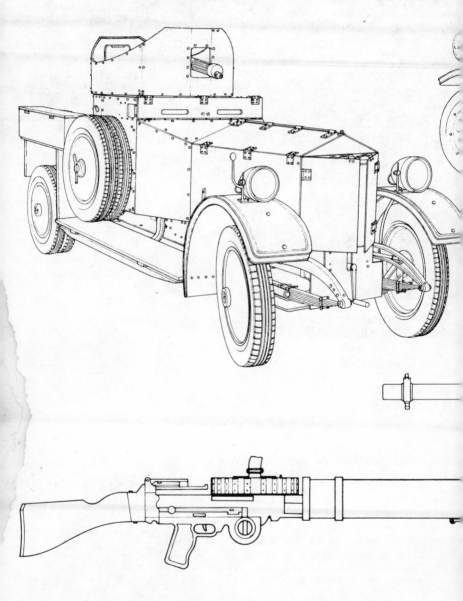

**British .303-inch Lewis light machine-gun**
*Calibre:* .303-inch. *Operation:* gas, automatic only. *Weight:* 27 lbs.
*Length overall:* 50½ inches. *Barrel length:* 26 inches. *Feed:* 47-round drum.
*Rate of fire:* 600 rounds per minute. *Muzzle velocity:* 2,440 feet per second

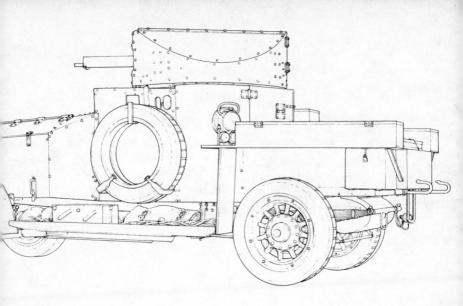

**tish Talbot armoured car**
**is** car was produced in 1914 on the 25hp Talbot chassis and had a turret
**ntical** with the Rolls-Royce armoured car. Its engine was not sufficiently
**werful** to give it the neccessary mobility, however, and after 1915 it were not
**ed** in the armoured role. Fitted with open box bodies it performed admirably
**a** tender

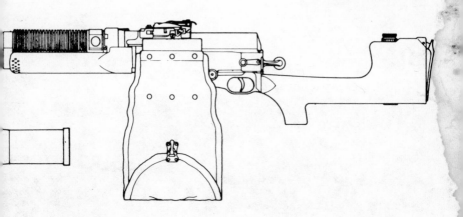

**nch 8mm M09/13 light machine-gun**
*libre:* 8mm. *Operation:* gas, selective fire. *Weight:* 27¼ lbs.
*ngth overall:* 46¾ inches. *Barrel length:* 35½ inches. *Feed:* 9, 14 or 30 round
*tal* strips. *Rate of fire:* 550 rounds per minute. *Muzzle velocity:* 2,500 feet
**r** second

uttling the lighters. Thus Lawrence
ad stopped the Dead Sea traffic a
ouple of weeks earlier than he had
riginally promised Allenby, when
ley had met at headquarters to
ake their post-Gaza plans.

Yet possibly because of sheer mental
nd physical fatigue, possibly in
eaction to the horror of Deraa, the
ext few weeks plunged Lawrence
nto growing gloom and despair. The
urkish strength was on the ebb, but
ach day seemed to reveal more and
lore to Lawrence's tortured mind
lat the Arabs were not either mili-
arily or emotionally capable of
aking advantage of the situation.
eisal had been sharply rebuffed
uring January in an attempt to
ake Mudauwara with a conventional
ttack of the kind Lawrence always
eprecated for the Bedouin; the
eather, bitterly cold, sapped all
leir strengths; to cap it all, Law-
ence discovered that the £30,000 in
old which he obtained from Aqaba
o act as a temporary treasury for
uture operations had been spent by
eid in a foolishly extravagant dis-
ursement to men who had not even
uffered the rigours of active service.
his last blow, in Lawrence's low
tate of mind, seemed more than he
ould baer. It was, he wrote bitterly,
he complete ruin of all my hopes
nd plans.' He decided to go to Beer-
heba, to tell Allenby that he could
o no more with the Arabs, and that
e had misjudged the situation. By
hance, on his way to headquarters,
e met Hogarth, then holding a naval
ank of commander, but in reality an
ntelligence chief in the Middle East.
etween them, Hogarth and Clayton,
ho was also present, convinced

afila, where the mere name of Auda had
aused the defenders to surrender.
ribal quarrels caused Auda to depart
vith his men, leaving the town
eriously under garrisoned

Lawrence that this was no moment
to resign. Allenby, too, when they
met, told Lawrence that the War
Cabinet in London were urging him
to the capture of Damascus. He
wanted the Arabs to assist him on
his right flank. Damascus was
Lawrence's dream, too.

'There was no escape for me,' he
said later. 'I must take up again my
mantle of fraud in the East . . . It
might be fraud or it might be farce:
no one should say that I could not
play it . . .'

Allenby's new plan involved an
attack north-east from Jerusalem by
the British forces, while the Arabs
advanced on Ma'an, protecting the
right flank. How far this 'protection'
can really have impressed Allenby is
very difficult to say. One must remember that Feisal's so-called 'regulars'
amounted to only about 600 men –
little more than an average British
battalion, and they were a good deal
less reliable. It seems probable that
Allenby was relying on the moral
effect produced on the Turks by
Lawrence's raiding operations, since
the weight of any conventional Arab
attack was necessarily restricted by
lack of first class training, and scar-
city of men on the ground. Certainly
in general, the Turks reacted mor
sharply to Lawrence than to Fe sal.
They now gave evidence of this by
promptly recapturing Tafila from
Zeid on 6th March.

Although the Arabs reoccupied
Tafila two weeks later, after the
Turks withdrew the garrison to
reinforce their forces in Amman,
there were difficult times ahead
Struggling through heavy rain
British troops occupied Salt, reaching
Amman itself on 27th March. However, the town had been reinforced
with two battalions – one German,
one Turkish – and the British attacked it in vain. When they withdrew, they also abandoned Salt. Wild
rumours began to sweep the Arab
fighters that the British were on the
run, that the Turks would soon be

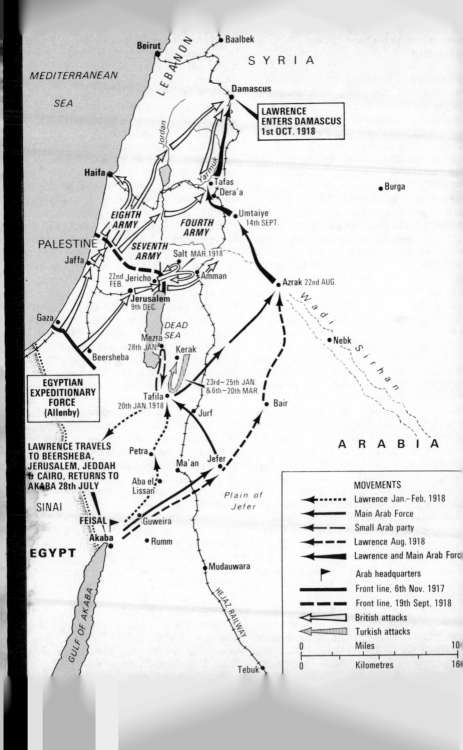

*bove:* Turkish observation post. *Below:* The Tafila garrison's commander, Zeid (centre), with captured Austrian-made Turkish guns

Arab 'regulars'. Frontal attacks by these troops prove very costly. Lawrence favoured tactics which would exploit the speed and mobility of the desert Arab

back in Jerusalem, and that in Salt they were hanging Arabs who had rallied to Feisal's cause. Meanwhile, the Arab 'regulars', attempting a conventional attack, had failed to take Ma'an. The assault on the Ma'an station, which had cost heavy casualties, was led by Nuri Said, who later became Prime Minister of Iraq.

Amid these gathering shadows, Lawrence was living in a world of labyrinthine, Byzantine intrigue. Feisal might, indeed, be an army commander under Allenby, but the words were words only. In reality, Feisal was pursuing objectives which were

British troops march through Salt at the beginning of their brief occupation

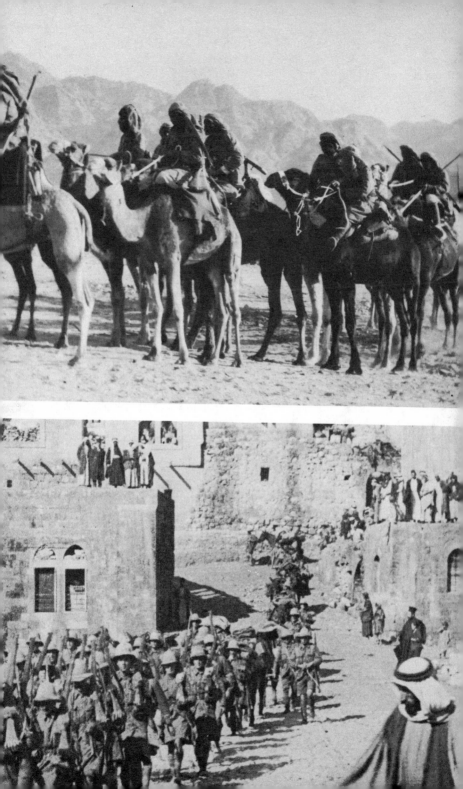

The disbanding of the Imperial Camel Corps released 2,000 camels for Lawrence's operations

separate from, and in some degree hostile to, the interests of Britain. Lawrence was becoming increasingly aware of the ambivalence of his position as a British officer amongst this alien people. However, Lawrence was not the only one with a foot in each camp. In the spring of 1918, Feisal was in communication with the Turks. Mohammed Said, the brother of the Abd el Kader who had deserted Lawrence on the ill-fated Yarmuk raid, had visited Feisal with an offer from Jemal Pasha for peace negotiations – a separate peace, that is, between Turks and Arabs. Although Feisal fenced and manoeuvred in letter after letter, the correspondence went on. Meanwhile, the British effort to the north, the success of which was the only sure way of holding Feisal's friendship relaxed. The German spring offensive in France, a critical moment on the Western Front, was drawing divisions from Allenby's 'sideshow'.

It was a curious chance which finally ended any thoughts Feisal entertained about a separate peace. Lawrence dined with Allenby at headquarters on 5th May. He had heard that much of the Imperial Camel Brigade was to be disbanded in Sinai. This would leave 2,000 riding camels available, and Lawrence wanted them. From Sir Walter Campbell, the Quartermaster-General, he received a dusty answer when he made his plea, but he raised the point again at dinner. Allenby asked him why he wanted them so urgently. Lawrence said boldly: 'To put a thousand men into Deraa any day I please.' Allenby turned to Campbell, smiled, and said: 'Q, you lose.'

Few more impressive gifts could have been devised. Feisal gasped with joy when he was told. It was a gift of mobility and power. Two thousand camels would take him to Damascus.

# Ashes of triumph

Turkish dead litter a road near Damascus

he character of the desert war was
hanging for Lawrence. More and
more British officers were arriving
r duties with the Arab regular and
regular forces. Lieutenant Ian Kirk-
ride (later to become British
inister in Amman); Captain Hornby,
the Royal Engineers, an expert on
molition; F G Peake, of the
gyptian Camel Corps, who was
ter to found the Arab Legion of
ransjordan; Colonel Alan Dawnay,
staff officer in charge of Mejaz
perations; armoured car comman-
rs, aircraft commanders, and many
hers. There was even some sort of
derstudy for Lawrence, a Captain
ubert Young, a fluent Arabic-
eaker and a regular soldier, of
hom Lawrence exhibited a rather
ildish jealousy. At this time,
awrence was in the full flow of his
le with the Arabs, exhibiting to
itish visitors a confident mastery
his position. Peake remembered
vidly his first meeting:

'The party was headed by a small
an dressed in extremely good and
pensive Bedouin clothes, a richly-
aided and decorated goat's hair
oak over all, and on his head a
onderful silk *kufaiyeh* (shawl) held
position by a gold *agal* (silk cord).
s feet were bare, and he had a gold
ejazi dagger in his belt, and in his
nd he carried the usual almond-
ood cane that every Bedouin camel-
ler uses. As this regal-looking
rson came through the tent door
th the light at his back, I imagined
must be the Emir Feisal himself
t for a stroll in the cool morning
, or, at least, a very important
essenger from him. I went, there-
e, to meet the distinguished
anger, and ceremoniously showed

him to a chair, speaking the usual
flowery Arabic words of the welcome
and greetings. He had barely sat down
when to my surprise he said in perfect
English: "Well, Peake, so you have
arrived at last. We have been waiting
some time for you and your braves,
and there is plenty of work for you
up country." I realized then that my
distinguished stranger was no other
than Lawrence himself . . .'

Perhaps to keep his dominance
among this gathering throng of com-
patriots, perhaps as a result of his
general hardening of personality after
Deraa, Lawrence became increasingly
reckless and ruthless. He joined with
Dawnay in armoured car operations
against railway stations and posts –
operations in which Dawnay, a
thorough, experienced, intelligent
regular became so successful that he
finally wrecked eighty miles of railway line between Ma'an and Mudauwara. By suppressing sentences in
angry telegrams between Feisal and
Husein, his jealous father in Mecca, he
averted a fatal split in the Sherifian
forces which would have ruined the
plan to seize Damascus. But it was in
his personal behaviour that the strain
was beginning to show. He was arro-
gant and conceited at headquarters,
vindictive and even cruel in battle.
And battle, more battle, was on the
way.

On the Western Front, the German
spring offensive had failed. Allenby's
moment for his own offensive was
drawing near. It was now planned to
launch it in September. The basis of
Allenby's plan was to foster in
Turkish minds the idea that he intended once more to batter the
British forces against Amman, east
of the River Jordan, whereas in
reality he intended to make his
breakthrough along the coast. Elaborate deception arrangements were
made to confuse the Turks as to the
real objectives. Headquarters was
moved from the coast to Jerusalem;
bridges and roads were built on and
round the River Jordan; tents and

ptain Hornby, a demolition expert of
Royal Engineers, with F G Peake,
yptian Camel Corps, who later
nded the Arab Legion of Transjordan
ese and many other British officers
re now arriving for the final stage of
Middle Eastern war

**Feisal leaving the Hotel Victoria after his interview with Allenby and Lawrence**

imitation horses were carefully arranged in the Jordan valley to deceive air reconnaissance, while the cavalry corps moved off by night to new positions nearer the coast.

Lawrence and the Arabs had an important part to play in Allenby's design. He wanted them to gnaw and worry at the Turkish left flank, east of the Jordan, and to cut the railway lines at Deraa. In some ways this well suited Lawrence and Feisal, for successful operations round Deraa would leave open the option of a quick dash to Damascus, rallying the local tribes on the way.

A considerable force was assembled at Azrak for the Arab part in Allenby operation. Lawrence had with him contingent of armoured cars; Fei his 'regulars', nearly 600 stro commanded by Nuri es-Said; Pea was there with his Egyptian Can Corps unit; Pisani with his mount battery; and all were supported some thousands of loot-hungry lo Bedouin tribesmen. In a series raids, culminating, ironically, in destruction of the great Yarm bridge at Tell el-Shehab which given such trouble the previc November, the Arabs cut the railw round the Deraa junction from nor south and west, completely interru

**Colonel Alan Dawnay, who joined with Lawrence in armoured car operations directed at the railways**

ing traffic to and from Palestine. They did the job with twenty-four hours to spare, for at dawn on 19th September, Allenby attacked, sweeping over the Turkish trenches, and letting the cavalry through to ride across the Turkish coastal lines of retreat. In part, at least, the enemy commander, Liman von Sanders, had been deceived by the elaborate deception plan, and by Lawrence's activities round Deraa, into believing that the main blow would come in the east.

With Allenby's destruction of the Turkish Seventh and Eighth Armi[es] in Palestine, Lawrence's main tas[k] now was to assist an Indian divisio[n] commanded by the Australia[n] General Barrow, in harrying a[nd] breaking up the Turkish Four[th] Army as it pulled back out of Amma[n] and retreated north towards Dera[a]. Barrow was instructed by Allenby n[ot] to try to implement his 'saucy threa[t]' to take Damascus until other Alli[ed] columns were positioned tcgether [to] enter the city. It was not an ord[er] to which Lawrence, in his prese[nt] mood, was likely to pay much atte[ntion]

Peake's Egyptian Camel Corps

on.
First, however, there was Deraa – a
ord of evil and horror in Lawrence's
cabulary. Possibly it was the
emory of what had happened at
eraa which drove Lawrence to a
uelly ruthless act. As they moved
pidly forward to the rail junction,
here the Germans were already
irning un-airworthy planes and sur-
us stores, it was realised that the
treating Turks would pass through
ifas, which happened to be the home
llage of one of Lawrence's friends,
illal. Not unnaturally, Tallal was

anxious, and the Arab column at-
tepted to reach Tafas before the
Turks. They were too late. When they
arrived at Tafas, they found the
village burning, and evidence of
atrocities by the Turks all around –
a woman obscenely pierced by a saw-
bayonet, dead children, more dead
women. Tallal could bear no more.
Drawing his headcloth about his face,
he rode to a position above the re-
treating rearguard and then charged
down at them, alone, shouting his

war-cry 'Tallal, Tallal', until he fell to a score of bullets. Vengefully but not unnaturally, the Arabs began butchering the Turkish wounded who lay along the roadside. They also wiped out a party of German and Austrian officers and machine gunners, killing every one. 'By my order,' said Lawrence, 'we took no prisoners, for the only time in our war . . .' Cruel and yet understandable in the circumstances, perhaps – but worse was to come.

After catching up with the fighting Turkish rearguard, they found a group of Arabs who had taken prisoner about 200 men, mostly Turks, though with a fair sprinkling of German service corps men. Nearby was an Arab who had been elaborately pinned with bayonets. Before he died, he nodded towards the shivering group of prisoners. This seems to have been enough for Lawrence. 'We turned our Hotchkiss on the prisoners and made an end of them,' he reported later. As to this, the killing of 200 men with a machine gun is not an easy matter. The scene, dismissed in suspiciously few words both in Lawrence's contemporary account, and in *Seven Pillars,* must have been indescribably revolting. It was something which any responsible officer had a duty to prevent – and certainly not to encourage. The whole sad affair was one more example of how Lawrence was beginning to slide into an abyss of personal crisis after Deraa.

Lawrence was at his infuriating worst when he met Barrow, a somewhat rigid Australian, in the shattered ruins of Deraa. He had reached the town some hours ahead of Barrow, and adopted a condescending tone in telling the divisional commander, who asked where he intended to spend the next night: 'In Damascus.' Meanwhile, all along the road to the city, Auda and his tribesmen were busy with an orgy of loot and slaughter of the disintegrating remnants of the Fourth Army. On 30th September, the last Turkish troops hurried north out of Damascus, which was now empty, inviting, ripe for plucking by the Arab cavalry and camelry. Unlimited mobility, as conferred by two thousand camels, has its advantages, for a man who is prepared to disobey orders.

At dawn on 1st October, riding in his Rolls Royce *Blue Mist*, with a British officer, Stirling, beside him, and the Sherif Nasir ahead on a horse, Lawrence entered Damascus. This, the triumph to which he had looked forward for so long, began in anticlimax and ended in bitter farce and disappointment. They rode in to faint cheers or sullen silence, from a people too bemused by the passing of a tide of war to comprehend clearly what was happening. In the centre of the city, beside the town hall, however, there was a more traditional welcome, a shouting crowd screaming their names, dervishes slashing themselves in ecstasy, a pulsating roar of excitement.

Inside the town hall, Lawrence received a numbing shock. Beside Nasir stood Abd el Kader, the Algerian who Lawrence believed had tried to betray him at the Yarmuk, and his brother, the Turkish negotiator Mohammed Said. With Shukri el Ayubi, a Damascus resistance leader who bore an honoured Arab name, they had formed a provisional government in the hours before Lawrence's arrival, proclaiming the Sherif Husein 'King of the Arabs'.

Even as Lawrence tried to deal with this situation, he was interrupted by a farcical event. Auda, standing in the jostling throng, had been insulted by a Druse sheik, and the two were now grappling in a murderous struggle. Helped by friends, Lawrence hauled Auda off the Druse. The old

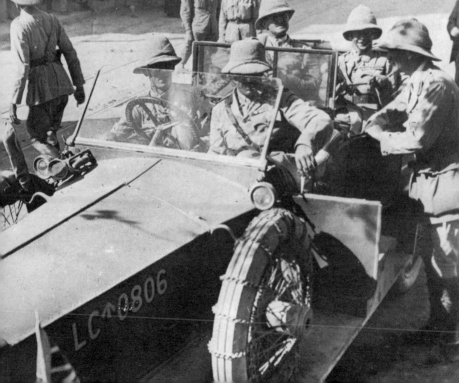

aider was foaming at the mouth, mad nd screaming, and while he was eing calmed, Abd el Kader and Iohammed Said vanished from the oom. It all seemed a poor augury for rab unity in the moment of victory.

Over the next three days, Lawrence ought to hold Damascus for Feisal. e had as opponents not only Abd el ader and Mohammed Said, but also ne suspicious Australian General arry Chauvel, whose cavalry had ntered the city at almost the same me as Lawrence himself. Chauvel, nderstandably, was none too sure hat Lawrence was not jumping the un in his attempts to set up an Arab lministration on behalf of Feisal. owever, he finally accepted, for the oment, Lawrence's claim that hukri el Ayabi was *de facto* acting overnor.

Meanwhile, Lawrence informed bd el Kader and Mohammed Said hat they were deposed. Mohammed aid jeered at him as a Christian fidel; Abd el Kader, lunatic as ever, ttacked him with a dagger. He was ung back by Auda, and the two rothers stalked angrily from the all. Lawrence was not finished with hem yet, however. That night he ook some loyal tribesmen to rush the ouse in which the brothers were aying. In a report made to Cairo ome months later, he said that he rrested Abd el Kader, meaning to noot him as soon as he laid hands on s brother, who was not there. How- er, before this could be done, Feisal rived and announced a general nnesty under which Abd el Kader as released. He was, in fact, shot ad by a sentry in the street soon

after Lawrence left Damascus.

Feisal was not the only great figure to have now reached Damascus. Allenby also arrived, on 3rd October, an hour or two before Feisal. He was none too pleased with what was happening. There was trouble with the French. He summoned Feisal to his headquarters at once, making it quite clear that he regarded Feisal as an officer under his command. In *Seven Pillars*, Lawrence is oblique about the conversation which now took place. The best account, partly ver- batim, comes in Chauvel's official report:

'Lawrence acted as interpreter. The Commander-in-Chief explained to Feisal:
a. That France was to be the Pro- tecting Power over Syria. b. That he, Feisal, as representing his father, King Husein, was to have the admini- stration of Syria (less Palestine and the Lebanon province) under French guidance and financial backing. c. That the Arab sphere would include the hinterland of Syria only, and that he, Feisal, would not have anything to do with the Lebanon . . . d. That he was to have a French liaison officer at once, who would work for the present with Lawrence, who would be expected to give him every assistance.

'Feisal objected very strongly. He said that he knew nothing of France in the matter; that he was prepared to have British assistance; that he understood from the adviser whom Allenby sent him that the Arabs were to have the whole of Syria including the Lebanon, but excluding Palestine; that a country without a port was no good to him, and that he declined to have a French liaison officer or to recognise French guidance in any way.

'The Chief turned to Lawrence and said: "But did you not tell him that the French were to have the Pro- tectorate over Syria?" Lawrence said: "No, sir, I know nothing about it." The Chief then said: "But you knew definitely that he, Feisal, was to have nothing to do with the

Allenby's arrival in Damascus on 3rd ctober caused Lawrence some nbarrassment – Feisal was told that awrence had known all along that ance was to be the Protecting Power Syria

Lebanon?" Lawrence said: "No, sir, I did not."

'After some further discussion, the Chief told Feisal that he, Sir Edmund Allenby, was Commander-in-Chief, and that he, Feisal, was at the moment a Lieutenant-General under his command and that he would have to obey orders. That he must accept the situation until the whole matter was settled at the conclusion of the war. Feisal accepted this decision and left with his entourage, except Lawrence.

'After Feisal had gone, Lawrence told the Chief that he would not work with a French liaison officer and that he was due for leave and thought he had better take it now and go off to England. The Chief said: "Yes, I think you had," and Lawrence left the room . . .'

He left Damascus immediately. Many reasons have been advanced for his sudden departure – war-weariness, a desire to get out before anti-climax set in, even, though highly unlikely, a wish to serve on the Western Front. Yet if Chauvel's account is true – and it must be admitted that it has the ring of reality – Lawrence could have done little else. This was the moment of truth. Whatever he said to Allenby, he had, of course, long known about the Sykes-Picot agreement and French plans for Syria. He was now in an impossible position. His career as a war leader was over. He might desire to take some part in Arab politics over the next crucial months or years, but he could hardly enter on this role now, as a lieutenant-colonel, under the cold, watchful eye of his commander-in-chief. If Feisal had to obey orders, so – even more so – did Lawrence. To stay with Feisal meant a weary period of lies and frustration. leading nowhere.

# The anti-climax

T E Lawrence, alias
Aircraftsman Shaw

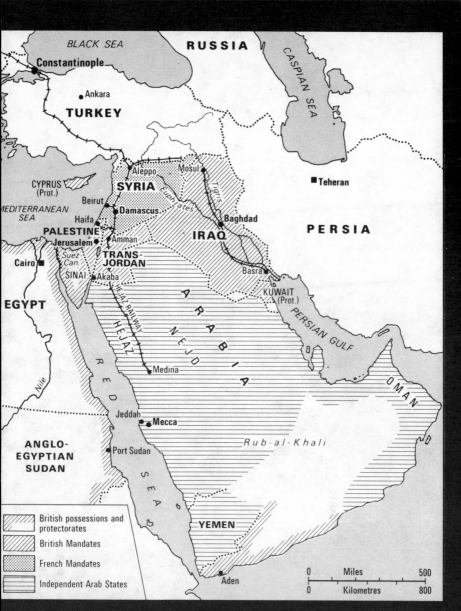

The Middle East. 1920

It was now, when all was over, that Lawrence achieved the fame that he had half-wanted, half-recoiled from. The lectures of the American journalist, Lowell Thomas, and the tremendous publicity of the popular newspapers, made him an almost-legendary hero – an Elizabethan figure whose daring and romantic war seemed to stand in such stark contrast to the grim miseries of the trenches of Flanders and the Somme. For a while he moved still with great affairs, accompanying Feisal – not altogether to the Emir's pleasure – to the Peace Conference after the war, irritating the French, still trying to make Feisal a king. In the end, much of his dream failed. True, Husein saw Feisal sit briefly upon the Syrian throne, and then on that of Iraq; while his other son, the lethargic Abdulla whom Lawrence had disliked became Emir and then King of Jordan. But the hated French secured from the League of Nations a mandate over Syria and Lebanon, while the British held another mandate over Palestine and the lands of Transjordan. First Peake, and later Glubb, built the Arab Legion, partly from the tradition of the Revolt, but it was not – especially in later years – a force with which Lawrance of Arabia would easily have identified.

Personal life, too, for Lawrence became an anticlimax. Half fascinated by conventional success, he veered uneasily from one extreme to the other. He liked the company of intellectuals – George Bernard Shaw, Ronald Storrs, David Garnett, Robert Graves. He seemed always to be able to act a part – a sort of chameleon, able to adapt his mental colours to anyone whom he was beside at the time. Yet he was always tortured by self-doubt – trying to 'escape' by joining, in the ranks, first the Royal Air Force, then the Tank Corps, then the RAF again. He longed to write

**Lawrence with Prince Feisal at the Paris peace conference in January 1919**

151

Glubb Pasha, who took over the
building of the Arab Legion from Peake

On 13th May 1935 T E Lawrence crashed
while riding his motorcycle; six days
later he died

Above: The scene of Lawrence's fatal accident. Below: Clouds Hill, where Lawrence was living at the time of his death. The building is now National Trust property, and preserves a room much as Lawrence left it. Right: Lawrence's brother with August John arrives at the inquest on the accident.

great book: in *Seven Pillars of Wisdom*, produced with matchless posturing and mystification, he achieved a good book, but one too self-conscious, too self-absorbed, but ultimately not self-revealing enough to be great. It is hard to imagine Lawrence as an old man. If he were alive today, he would be advancing to his eighties. However, that was not to be. On 13th May, 1935, riding his motor bicycle at Clouds Hill, Dorset, he swerved to avoid two schoolboys, and crashed into a tree. His brain was irreparably damaged, and six days later he died.

It would be idle to deny that in Lawrence, behind the play-acting, the self-absorption, even the lies, there was a tremendous triumph of will, of mind over body, of intellectual driving force working on a field of action. Aqaba alone was an achievement such as few men have to their credit. The whole handling of Feisal and the Arabs, and their brilliant use as an instrument of war, seem hardly to have been within the scope of any other individual. Lawrence may not have been, as Liddell Hart believed, a great captain, in the histrocial sense of those words. But he was certainly a great leader – a man who could make other men willingly accomplish dangerous, difficult, uncomfortable things. More than that, he could cast a spell – as those who came under it, from Winston Churchill to army privates, have testified. He had the remarkable quality of convincing

The funeral at Moreton in Dors

those whom he wished to attach to to himself that his friendship was precious. Even across half a century, reading *Seven Pillars of Wisdom,* or the Lawrence letters, or the wartime reports, it is still possible to get, without ever having seen him, a strong feeling that it would be pleasant to be held high in his regard. That was his secret in Arabia, and that, amongst many famous and influential people, was the quality which kept him always, in spite of his elaborate renunciations and escapes, at the edge of the forefront of great affairs. On the very day he died, he had ridden into Bovington to answer a telegram from a friend who proposed that he should meet Hitler.

However, it is as Lawrence of Arabia that he lives in British memory. In the Dorest church of St Martin's at Wareham he lies in stone effigy, like one of the Crusaders whose castles he had studied before he fought his war. His head rests on a camel saddle: he wears the Bedouin cloak and headress, and the knotted *agal*. His dagger is sheathed; his camel whip lies beside him. By his head are three books – the Oxford Book of English Verse, Malory's Morte d'Arthur, and the Greek Anthology, which he had carried with him in the desert.

In the churchyard at Moreton, his tombstone bears the words: *Dominus Illuminatio Mea* – 'God My Light'. They are, of course, the motto of his University of Oxford, but for Lawrence they do not seem appropriate. One might find a better epitaph for him from the Arabs whom he half-loved, half-hated, as in those lines from al-Mutanabbi, the mediaeval Arab poet:

> 'Night and the horse and the desert knew me,
> And sword and lance, and paper and pen.'

# Bibliography

*Seven Pillars of Wisdom,* by T E Lawrence. Cape (1940 edn.).
*T E Lawrence by his Friends* (ed. A W Lawrence). Cape, 1937.
*T E Lawrence: In Arabia and After,* by B H Liddell Hart. Cape, 1934.
*The Secret Lives of Lawrence of Arabia,* by Phillip Knightley and Colin Simpson
Nelson, 1969.
*T E Lawrence: An Arab View,* by Suleiman Mousa. Oxford University Press, 196
*Lawrence of Arabia: The Man and the Motive,* by Anthony Nutting. Hollis and
Carter, 1961.
*Orientations,* by Ronald Storrs. Nicholson and Watson, 1937.
*Arab Command: the Biography of Lieut Col F G Peake Pasha,* by Major C S Jarvis
Hutchinson, 1943.
*Lawrence of Arabia: An Historical Appreciation,* by Erik Lonnroth. Valentine,
Mitchell, 1956.
*The Arabs,* by P K Mitti. Macmillan, 1948.
*Britain and the Arabs,* by Lieut General Sir John Bagot Glubb. Hodder and
Stoughton, 1959.
*Lawrence of Arabia: a Biographical Enquiry,* by Richard Aldington. Collins, 195£
Grateful acknowledgment is made to Jonathan Cape Ltd, and to Doubleday ar
Co, New York, for permission to quote certain passanges from *Seven Pillars of
Wisdom.*